The JOY of FOOD

Celebrating the Role Food Plays in Our Lives

Published by

Cheryl Alfrey Waldeck

Tulsa, Oklahoma

For three special women who have graced my life:
My mother Gladys Alleen Adams Alfrey,
and my grandmother
Nellie Amanda Hartsfield Alfrey, who were my earliest
cooking instructors and whose memory continues to
inspire me; and for my mother-in-law
Betty Lou Shaffer Waldeck, a masterful cook
and hostess.

Cover Design By

Carl Brune

First Printing: February 2015
Available: Amazon.com/books, or cherwaldeck@cox.net

What is it about food that brings us closer together?

It is more than for mere sustenance. Sharing a meal creates an atmosphere of nourishment and gladness that sustains both body and soul. When we make time to bake a birthday cake or prepare a well-loved dish, we are expressing affection, creating and preserving memories and taking pause for thankfulness.

The inspiration for this book has come from a lifetime of joyous celebrations at tables filled with delicious food, beloved family and special friends. Each recipe evokes a memory and has its own story to tell. In addition to savory creations like Prime Rib in Rock Salt and my comforting Chicken Pot Pie, you will find time-honored family specialties like Gladdie's Pie Crust, Grandma Alfrey's Banana Nut Bread and Fourth of July Waldeck Ice Cream. Every dish is sure to create heartfelt memories for you as well.

You will also find the art of entertaining made easy with tips for pairing food with wine, setting a genteel table, utilizing flowers in creative ways, and crafting menus that will allow you to enjoy the party as much as your guests. There are recipes for both the experienced and novice accompanied by cooking techniques, baking secrets, and how-to instruction for developing good cooking habits and stocking the kitchen and pantry.

From salty to sweet and cocktails to cookies, **The Joy of Food** *holds something just right to nurture and celebrate every person and occasion in life. From my table to yours – let these recipes celebrate the role food plays in all our lives and yield memories worth savoring.*

TABLE OF CONTENTS

Cocktails & Appetizers

COCKTAILS
Anniversary Alexanders
Kentucky Mint Juleps
Legend's Lemon Drop Martinis
Spanish Sangria

APPETIZERS
Black-Eyed Susans
Perfect Bites
Priceless Lobster in Corn Husks
Salsa Fresca
Sherried Mushroom Strudel
Supreme Artichoke Squares

Anniversary Alexanders

It is hard to find a bartender who knows how to make a good Alexander, so we often make these at home. The secret is to use ice cream as opposed to ice. Beginning with our 1982 honeymoon in Bermuda, this after-dinner treat has become a wedding anniversary tradition for Todd and me.

Yield: Four drinks

2 jiggers brandy
1 jigger crème de cocao
½ cup milk

1 pint vanilla bean ice cream
Nutmeg

- ♥ Put all ingredients (except nutmeg) into blender and blend briefly until smooth but still thick in consistency.
- ♥ Pour into brandy snifter and sprinkle lightly with nutmeg.
- ♥ Add a straw and serve immediately.

Kentucky Mint Juleps

While attending the University of Kentucky in Lexington, I learned to appreciate the traditions and trappings of horse racing. **My brother Sam and sister Jane** *(Off to the races in 1979 at left) also attended UK, and each fall we enjoyed boxed seats at Keeneland Thoroughbred Racing Park thanks to friends Angie and Guy. At Keeneland, all gentlemen are required to wear a tie, or one will be provided. We loved Kentucky and the experience of being in the old south, where making a good Mint Julep on race day was also required. This is how I was taught to make a Mint Julep in Kentucky.*

Yield: One Julep

1 silver julep cup   **Granulated sugar**
Finely crushed ice   **Good Kentucky bourbon**
Fresh mint leaves

- ♥ Take a silver julep cup—only a silver cup. Fill it with ice crushed to the fineness of snow.
- ♥ Bruise one tender leaf of mint to extract its essence, and add it to the ice.
- ♥ Then dissolve a teaspoon of sugar in a Kentucky jigger of good bourbon whisky and pour over ice. Let the fluid filter through the ice to the bottom of the cup.
- ♥ Swirl the cup slowly until a coating of a thick white frost forms on the outside. Garnish with a sprig of mint and hand to an appreciative lady or gentleman.

THE JULEP CUP

A traditional mint julep is served in silver or pewter cups, and is held only by the bottom and top edges, allowing frost to form on the outside of the cup.

Legend's Lemon Drop Martinis

*This cocktail is served only to "legendary" ladies. These martinis are sweet and strong, just like my friends. At left are **the original Legends** who attend my annual celebrations for dynamic, accomplished women – and who are always properly accessorized!*

Yield: Two martinis

1/3 cup juice of fresh lemon
2 Tablespoons granulated sugar
2 jiggers Absolut citron vodka,
frozen

6 fresh mint leaves
Ice, crushed
Martini shaker
Martini glasses, frosted

- ♥ Rinse mint and allow to dry naturally.
- ♥ Fill martini shaker to half way mark with crushed ice.
- ♥ Add lemon juice, sugar, vodka and mint leaves; shake vigorously until well combined.
- ♥ Pour into frosted martini glasses with the rims coated lightly with sugar (optional) and garnish with a sprig of fresh mint. Voilà!

NOTE: Squeeze a generous amount of fresh lemon juice in advance of the party and dilute slightly with cool water; refrigerate until ready to use.

Spanish Sangria

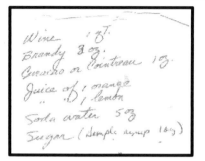

*This recipe originated in Madrid Spain where my mother-in-law coaxed the waiter in a local cantina to write out the ingredients on a **napkin** in 1967 (pictured at left). I have since embellished the original recipe and added fresh peaches and arugula.*

Yield: Twelve drinks

2 bottles inexpensive cabernet wine
½ cup brandy
¼ cup Cointreau or orange liqueur
¼ cup simple syrup
Juice of 1 orange

Juice of 1 lemon
2 peaches, sliced
4 cups arugula, cleaned
5 ounces soda water

- ♥ Mix wine, brandy, liqueur and simple syrup in a large pitcher.
- ♥ Add juices and fruit. Stir in the arugula and crush with a spoon to release the flavors.
- ♥ Cover and refrigerate for **6 to 12 hours**.
- ♥ Stir in soda, strain and serve in chilled glasses over ice.

SIMPLE SYRUP

Simple syrup is simply sugar and water that has been reduced to a syrup consistency.

Make simple syrup by boiling together equal parts sugar and water until the sugar dissolves.

OPTIONAL: Add strips of orange and lemon rind to the mixture as it boils. Let cool before using.

Black-Eyed Susans

I love to serve these treats in the fall. The savory cheese cookie with the sweetness of dates and crunch of toasted almonds is a delightful combination. These cookies are easy to make, but stuffing the dates takes a bit of time. Sit down for the task and, "Make a game of it," as my mother used to say.

Yield: Thirty-two cookies

4 ounces sharp cheddar cheese, grated
½ cup butter, chilled
1 cup all-purpose flour
2 Tablespoons fresh parmesan cheese

¼ teaspoon kosher salt
1/8 teaspoon ground red pepper
16 whole dates, pitted & halved lengthwise
32 whole blanched almonds
Freshly ground black pepper

- ♥ Preheat oven to 350 degrees.
- ♥ In a food processor bowl, process cheese and butter until combined. Gradually add the flour, processing until combined. Add the parmesan, salt, and red pepper. Process until well combined.
- ♥ Form the mixture into two logs, about 1-inch in diameter and 8-inches long. Wrap in plastic wrap and refrigerate about **1 hour** or until firm. While dough is chilling, stuff each date half with an almond and set aside.
- ♥ Slice logs into ¼-inch slices. Shape each slice of dough into a boat shape with your fingers. Wrap around the bottom and up to the cut edge of each almond-stuffed date, with the almond on top. Place bites on a baking sheet and sprinkle with black pepper.
- ♥ Bake 10 minutes or until golden brown.
- ♥ Remove and cool slightly on a wire rack. Serve warm.

NOTE: Bites can be made ahead and chilled or frozen (up to one month) until ready to serve. Then just reheat at 350 degrees for 5 minutes or until heated through.

Perfect Bites

These appetizers are a favorite. The sweet basil and goat cheese combined with crunchy pine nuts make a perfectly combined bite.

Yield: Twenty "perfect" bites

½ cup pine nuts, lightly toasted
4 ounces soft goat cheese, at room temperature
2 Tablespoons half and half cream
Kosher salt

Freshly ground black pepper
20 large unblemished basil leaves
2 medium plum tomatoes, finely chopped
Extra-virgin olive oil (for drizzling)

♥ Toast pine nuts in a small skillet over medium heat, stirring occasionally, for approximately 3 minutes. This is the best way to roast this buttery soft nut. Stir and turn nuts as they roast and watch carefully to ensure they do not burn. Let cool.
(See additional tips for *Toasting Nuts & Seeds* on following page.)

♥ Wash basil leaves and allow to dry naturally on paper towel. (Choose large, 2 to 3-inch leaves.) Finely chop tomatoes.

♥ In a small bowl, mix the goat cheese with half and half and season lightly with salt and pepper. Dollop 1 teaspoon of the cheese on each basil leaf; placing bites on serving plate as you go.

♥ Sprinkle the pine nuts evenly onto each dollop, lightly pressing nuts into the cheese to set. Scatter the chopped tomatoes on each bite; pressing lightly to set as well.

♥ Drizzle bites lightly with good quality olive oil. Top with freshly ground black pepper.

♥ Serve immediately, and be prepared for these to go fast!

NOTE: Perfect Bites can be partially prepared 1 to 2 hours ahead of serving, by completing the first 3 steps. Just before guests arrive complete the remaining steps to ensure the nuts do not become soggy or the tomato juices run.

TOASTING NUTS & SEEDS

*Toasting brings out the essential oils in nuts and seeds,
resulting in much more flavor.
It is an easy process, and you are sure to notice the difference in taste.*

To toast nuts, place them on a baking sheet in a 350 degree oven
until they are fragrant and slightly brown, approximately 5 to 10 minutes
depending on the size of nut.

Smaller, less dense seeds and nuts such as cumin, pepitas (sunflower seeds) or
peppercorns, as well as pine nuts, are best toasted in a dry skillet over medium
high heat so they can be closely watched to prevent burning.
Toast seeds and nuts until aromatic and slightly brown, about 3 to 5 minutes.

Priceless Lobster in Corn Husks

This recipe has been adapted from one served in a well-known café in Santa Fe. The first time my husband and I went to this famed establishment we were newly married and on a limited income. When the waiter brought us the menus, Todd looked over the choices (and prices) very quietly. He then leaned in to me and stated that we could either order only appetizers, or leave, because we could not afford a full meal. We opted to stay for appetizers, and this is what I ordered - worth every penny!

Yield: Serves four

1 cup unsalted butter
1 teaspoon vanilla bean
1 teaspoon pure vanilla extract
5 cups lightly salted water
2 pounds fresh lobster meat

½ pound scallops
½ cup corn kernels, cooked
8 large corn husks
16 basil leaves, cut into chiffonade

- ♥ Preheat grill.
- ♥ Soak corn husks in hot water until pliable, about 15 minutes.
- ♥ Cream together the butter, vanilla bean and extract.
- ♥ Parboil the lobster in the water until three-quarters done (15 to 18 minutes). Cool and slice.
- ♥ Divide scallops, lobster and corn evenly between corn husks; top with 2 Tablespoons of creamed vanilla butter.
- ♥ Roll and tie the corn husks, securing with string at both ends as per instructions on following page.
- ♥ Grill until scallops are cooked, about 6 to 8 minutes. Be careful not to let the butter leak out while grilling. Serve immediately.

GARNISH: Fresh basil leaves.

FORMING TAMALES

Tamales are like little presents, and formed much like
wrapping and tying a box.

- ♥ Start by soaking husks in hot water until soft and pliable, about 15 minutes.
- ♥ Then separate corn husks into two piles, large and small.
- ♥ Tear the smaller pieces into strips approximately 6 x ¼-inches. Set aside.
- ♥ Lay out one (larger) husk with the narrow part pointed away.
- ♥ Place filling in the center area of the square.
- ♥ Fold one side of the tamale over the other to cover the filling.
- ♥ Then roll the folded husk up (lengthwise) completely, but loosely.
- ♥ Fold the top over and tie it with a bow with one of the thin strips created from smaller husks.
- ♥ Secure the bottom end with a second strip and bow.

Salsa Fresca

*Kids love Mexican food, and **my sons** have been crazy about salsa with chips and burritos from early on. This Tex Mex salsa works great for my family because you can make it hot, medium or mild, depending on the amount of jalapeño.*

Yield: One quart of salsa – enough to feed a crowd

3 cups ripe tomatoes, diced
1 yellow onion, diced
1/3 cup scallions, chopped (including green parts)
¼ cup fresh cilantro, minced
½ 15-ounce can crushed tomatoes

½ 15-ounce can whole peeled tomatoes, chopped
1 4-ounce can green chilies, minced
4 large cloves garlic, minced
1 teaspoon kosher salt
2 jalapeňo peppers, minced

- ♥ In a large mixing bowl, combine fresh tomatoes, onions and cilantro.
- ♥ Add canned tomatoes, chilies, garlic and salt. Stir gently to combine.
- ♥ Add jalapenos to taste and combine.

Sherried Mushroom Strudel

Mushrooms, butter and curry wrapped in crispy phyllo dough make it hard to leave room for the entrée!

Yield: Serves twelve

¾ cup unsalted butter
6 cups mushrooms, chopped fine
(any variety, or a mix)
1 teaspoon kosher salt
¼ teaspoon curry powder
6 Tablespoons sherry
2 shallots, minced

1 cup sour cream
1 cup plus 3 Tablespoons
homemade bread crumbs
8 sheets phyllo dough
Fresh chives &
Dollops of sour cream for garnish

- ♥ Melt ¼ cup butter in skillet over medium low heat. Add mushrooms, salt, curry powder, sherry and shallots. Sauté until mushrooms are wilted and liquid is evaporated, about 20 minutes. Cool.
- ♥ Stir in 1 cup sour cream and 3 Tablespoons bread crumbs. **Refrigerate mixture overnight**.
- ♥ Preheat oven to 375 degrees.
- ♥ Melt remaining ½ cup butter. Brush a sheet of phyllo with melted butter and sprinkle with bread crumbs. Repeat until there are four layers. Spread half the mushroom mixture evenly onto phyllo, leaving a 1-inch border. Roll lengthwise, jellyroll fashion.
- ♥ Brush completed roll with butter and sprinkle with bread crumbs.
- ♥ Place on lightly greased cookie sheet. Mark 8 equal slices with a sharp knife.
- ♥ Repeat the above process using remaining mushroom filling and phyllo. Bake strudels until lightly browned, approximately 40 minutes.

GARNISH: Small dollop of sour cream and chopped fresh chives.

Supreme Artichoke Squares

These cheesy squares get their zing from a few dashes of tabasco sauce. They are terrific for parties and delicious served hot, but need a small plate because of the oil content. This recipe can also be made ahead and frozen just before baking. On the day of your party, thaw in the refrigerator (1 to 2 hours) and then bake and cut into squares as directed. These versatile squares can also be wrapped in foil and reheated.

Yield: Serves six to eight

2 6-ounce jars marinated artichoke hearts
4 scallions, finely chopped (including green parts)
2 cloves garlic, minced
4 large eggs, slightly beaten
¼ cup buttery crackers, crushed
¼ teaspoon kosher salt

¼ teaspoon freshly ground black pepper
1 Tablespoon fresh oregano, minced
6 dashes tabasco sauce
½ pound sharp cheddar cheese, grated
2 Tablespoons parsley, minced

- ♥ Preheat oven to 325 degrees.
- ♥ Drain marinade from 1 jar of artichoke hearts into frying pan. Sauté scallions and garlic in marinade. Drain second jar of artichokes, discarding marinade. Press all artichoke hearts between paper towels to remove excess liquid. Chop finely and set aside.
- ♥ Combine eggs, crackers and seasonings. Stir in cheese, parsley, artichoke hearts, scallions and garlic and mix well.
- ♥ Spread mixture evenly in greased 7 x 11-inch pan. Bake for 30 minutes.
- ♥ Cut into squares. Serve immediately.

Soups &
Salads

SOUPS

Garden Tomato Bisque

Mom's Vegetable Soup

White Bean Twist

SALADS

Decedent Waldorf Salad

Heart Salad

Hearty Kale Salad

Roasted Asparagus & Fried Egg

Strawberry Spinach Salad,

Caramelized Pecans & Poppy Seed Dressing

Garden Tomato Bisque

This bisque is a wonderful way to use garden fresh tomatoes, onions and herbs. Served cold, it is delicious with warm Cheddar and Chive Biscuits or Crunchy Corn Biscuits. (See both recipes under Breads.*)*

Yield: Serves six

6 vine-ripened tomatoes
1 medium onion, sliced thin
2 Tablespoons unsalted butter
2 bay leaves
2 Tablespoons packed brown sugar
2 whole cloves
1 teaspoon kosher salt
½ teaspoon freshly ground black pepper

2 cups half and half cream
1 cup skim milk
2 Tablespoons fresh chives, chopped fine
2 Tablespoons fresh basil, chopped fine
Fresh parsley, minced
Pepitas, toasted

- ♥ Peel and chop tomatoes. Sauté onion in butter until soft. Add tomatoes, bay leaf, brown sugar, cloves, salt, pepper and basil.
- ♥ Simmer, stirring occasionally, until tomatoes are thoroughly cooked, about 25 minutes.
- ♥ Remove and discard bay leaf and cloves. Transfer mixture to food processor and purée. Blend in cream and milk.
- ♥ **Chill several hours or overnight.**
- ♥ Serve in chilled bowls and garnish with toasted pepitas and minced parsley.

HOW TO CLEAN LEEKS

It is important to carefully clean leeks because sand and dirt can become trapped in their many layers.

To enjoy the earthy, slightly sweet onion flavor of leeks, start by trimming the root portion, just above the base. Then slice off the fibrous green tops from the point where they begin to separate and spread out from the root. Discard the greens to compost bin. Slice the leek lengthwise and chop.

At this point, place chopped pieces in a colander and rinse thoroughly. Gently stir the leeks with your hands to dislodge any sand.
Then drain and cook as directed.

Mom's Vegetable Soup

This soup has always been a favorite. It's easy to make, hearty and healthy. My mom always served this soup with saltine crackers, and then peach pie. When I would come home from college or for a visit, I always asked mother to have vegetable soup and peach pie ready. Mmm, mmm, home.

Yield: Serves ten to twelve

1½ to 2-pound eye of round roast beef
¼ cup all-purpose flour
1 Tablespoon kosher salt
½ Tablespoon freshly ground black pepper
1 to 3 Tablespoons vegetable oil (dependent on the amount of fat in roast)
1 onion, chopped
2 garlic cloves, minced
8 carrots, sliced
8 celery stalks, sliced

4 potatoes, cubed
1 28-ounce can whole tomatoes
3 cups beef broth
1 cup water
2 Tablespoons fresh oregano (or 2 teaspoons dried)
3 bay leaves
3 Tablespoons kosher salt
1½ Tablespoons freshly ground black pepper
1 16-ounce bag frozen corn kernels
3/4 head cabbage, cored & sliced

- ♥ Coat the bottom of a large stock pot with vegetable oil and heat. Mix flour, salt and pepper and coat beef. Brown beef on all sides in oil.
- ♥ While beef is browning, prepare onion, garlic, carrots, celery and potatoes. Chop and slice vegetables into uniform ½-inch cubes and coins.
- ♥ Continue cooking beef; add onions, garlic, carrots, celery, potatoes; mix to combine. Add tomatoes, broth and water, along with spices; lower heat to simmer. Simmer covered for **three hours**.
- ♥ Remove beef from pot and cube into ½-inch pieces, removing fat as you go. Return to pot and bring to a boil. Core and slice cabbage into ½-inch cubes. Add corn and cabbage and season with additional salt to taste. Cook for **another hour**.

OPTIONAL: For a more earthy broth, leeks can be substituted for onion.

White Bean Twist

This hearty white bean soup is made a bit healthier by substituting kale for the traditional choice of ham. This twist makes the soup visually appealing via the touch of green, and adds a "super food" to the meal. Great for a cold winter day!

Yield: Serves ten to twelve

1 Tablespoon olive oil
1 Tablespoon garlic, minced
1 yellow onion, chopped
1½ quarts chicken broth
2 15-ounce cans cannellini beans, un-drained
2 15-ounce cans navy beans, un-drained

8 small red potatoes with skin on, cubed
6 carrots, sliced into coins
6 stalks celery, sliced
3 Tablespoon kosher salt, or to taste
1 teaspoon freshly ground black pepper
½ pound fresh kale

- ♥ In a large Dutch oven, heat oil, add garlic, and cook for approximately 1 minute, stirring constantly to avoid burning.
- ♥ Add onion and cook another 10 minutes, or until soft.
- ♥ Add chicken broth, beans, potatoes, carrot, celery, salt and pepper.
- ♥ Bring to a boil, then reduce heat and simmer for 1 hour, stirring occasionally.
- ♥ Taste broth and add more salt if necessary. Remove ribs from kale and chop into bite-sized pieces; set aside under damp paper towel.
- ♥ Just before serving, add kale and stir to cook for just 2 to 3 minutes or until tender.

NOTE: This soup is even better the second day. It also freezes well.

Decadent Waldorf Salad

As a girl, my family always enjoyed Sunday dinner. The weekly tradition included Grandma Alfrey, the counting of blessings and a leisurely game of scrabble after the dishes were done. Grandma and mother were good friends and enjoyed cooking together for their family. My sister and I were the sous chefs and salad makers, and Waldorf Salad was my favorite to both make and eat! Neither of the Alfrey women would have used brandy in their sauce, but I find it adds a bit of decadence.

Yield: Serves eight to ten

SALAD

6 jonathan apples, cored & chopped
2 crisp celery stalks, sliced diagonally

1 bunch seedless red grapes, halved
1½ cups toasted pistachios, chopped

- ♥ Combine fruit and celery and gently mix to combine. Set aside.
- ♥ Reserve pistachios until ready to serve.

FRESH FRUITY DRESSING

1 cup sour cream
½ cup light mayonnaise
1/3 cup granulated sugar

½ cup orange juice, freshly squeezed
1/8 cup juice of fresh lemon
2 jiggers brandy

- ♥ Mix all ingredients until creamy.
- ♥ Pour over fruit mixture and refrigerate for 1 to 2 hours.
- ♥ Add pistachios just before serving.

Heart Salad

This composed salad makes a beautiful presentation and the texture combination is really unusual. I like to serve at Christmas time and garnish with red pepper holly leaves.

Yield: Serves ten to twelve

1 bunch leaf lettuce or fresh kale
1 15-ounce can hearts of palm, sliced
1 15-ounce can artichoke hearts, quartered
1 cup walnuts, toasted & chopped

8 ounces roquefort cheese, crumbled
1 bunch scallions, chopped (including green parts)
1 pound mushrooms, sliced
Vinaigrette dressing (See recipe with *Hearty Kale Salad*)

- ♥ Outline a large serving tray with whole lettuce or kale leaves. Remove stems and tear remaining leaves into bite-sized pieces; add to center of tray.
- ♥ Arrange in five horizontal strips: ½ artichokes, ½ mushrooms, hearts of palm, remaining mushrooms, and remaining artichokes.
- ♥ Top with five vertical strips: ½ walnuts, ½ roquefort, green onions, remaining roquefort, and remaining walnuts.
- ♥ Sprinkle sparingly with vinaigrette just before serving.

GARNISH: Red pepper cut in the shape of holly leaves and set into inverted yellow rose petals.

OPTIONAL: Walnuts and roquefort can be substituted with pecans and provolone cheese for a milder salad.

Hearty Kale Salad

*This salad is loaded with super foods and will stick to your ribs and make you feel healthy and full all day long! The vinaigrette recipe is **my son Michael's.***

NOTE: *Vinaigrettes can be adapted to your own tastes. Just stick to the basic formula of 2 parts fat to 1 part acid then spice and flavor as per your preference.*

Yield: Serves six to eight

SALAD

1 bunch kale
1 yellow beet, grated
4 to 6-ounces goat cheese, crumbled

½ cup almonds, toasted & chopped
Rind of lemon, shaved

- ♥ Remove ribs from kale and chop into bite-sized pieces.
- ♥ Toss all ingredients thoroughly. Set aside.

MICHAEL'S VINAIGRETTE DRESSING

2 cloves garlic, minced
1/8 cup red onion, sliced paper thin
Juice of 1/2 fresh lemon
2 Tablespoons red wine vinegar

Kosher salt &
Freshly ground black pepper
½ cup olive oil

- ♥ Slice onion and chop into 1-inch pieces. Mix garlic, onion and lemon juice with vinegar. Season with salt and pepper.
- ♥ Drizzle olive oil into garlic mixture, whisking as you add.

HOW TO TRIM KALE & SWISS CHARD

The first step to enjoying Kale and Swiss Chard to remove the stems, which can be tough and stringy even when cooked.
Start by removing the stem from the center of the leaf by folding each leaf in half. With the back of the leaf on the outside, cut away the center vein in a V-shape. Wash greens in cool water and pat dry.

Roasted Asparagus & Fried Egg Salad

This is a wonderful luncheon salad. I like to serve this on the patio in the spring, when asparagus is at its peak. Remember the adage, "Seasonal foods are always a good choice because 'delicious' is best served fresh!"

Yield: Serves four

Arugula lettuce mix
4 small wedges of soft creamy cheese, such as havarti or Swiss
Freshly made vinaigrette dressing
1 pound fresh asparagus
Olive oil

Kosher salt &
Freshly ground black pepper
8 slices prosciutto
4 large eggs
2 to 3 Tablespoons butter

- ♥ Preheat oven to 400 degrees.
- ♥ Wash asparagus and break off woody parts of stems. Then place asparagus in a single layer on a cookie sheet and drizzle with olive oil. Season lightly with salt and pepper. Roast for 10 minutes, or until the stalks are tender but crisp and stems begin to brown.
- ♥ While asparagus is roasting, place the prosciutto in a single layer on another pan and roast (with asparagus) for 5 minutes.

TO COOK THE EGGS

- ♥ Melt butter in a medium-sized skillet over medium heat and wait until the bubbles die down. Crack the eggs into the skillet, taking care to keep them separate. Cook low and slow until the whites are cooked but the yolks are still slightly runny. Baste the yolks with pan butter as they cook. Cook eggs sunny side up – do not flip.

ASSEMBLY

- ♥ Divide lettuce onto 4 serving plates and place one wedge of cheese onto each bed. Lightly drizzle vinaigrette onto lettuce.
- ♥ Divide the asparagus and prosciutto evenly and place on each plate atop lettuce. Top with eggs & serve immediately with crusty bread.

Strawberry Spinach Salad

This spring salad is a light combination of sweet and tart.

Yield: Serves four to six

1 bunch fresh spinach
1 cup celery, sliced diagonally

1 pint strawberries, quartered
Rind of lemon, shaved

- ♥ Wash spinach and remove stems. Slice celery and berries. Shave lemon.
- ♥ Plate spinach; sprinkle with celery and strawberries; refrigerate.
- ♥ Assemble dressing and caramelize pecans.
- ♥ Drizzle salad with dressing; sprinkle with pecans; toss gently, top with lemon

Poppy Seed Dressing

½ **cup granulated sugar**
2 teaspoons salt
2 teaspoons dry mustard
2/3 cup vinegar

4 scallions, minced (including
green parts)
1½ **cups vegetable oil**
3 Tablespoons poppy seeds

- ♥ Combine sugar, salt, mustard, vinegar and scallions in a food processor.
- ♥ Slowly add the oil and process until thickened, 1 to 2 minutes.
- ♥ Stir in poppy seeds and refrigerate.

Betty's Caramelized Pecans

*Beautiful **Betty "O"** was a good friend of my mother's and a wonderful cook. She appreciated good food, but also wanted to be able to water ski or sit in the sun with friends as opposed to spending all day in the kitchen. She was a woman after my own heart! These pecans are a great example of her easy cooking style, and are delicious on salad or eaten alone as a snack.*

1 egg white

1 pound pecans

1 cup sugar

½ teaspoon cinnamon

1 brown paper bag

- ♥ Preheat oven to 200 degrees.
- ♥ Beat egg white with a fork until frothy; pour over pecans and stir until all nuts are coated. Mix sugar and cinnamon until well combined.
- ♥ Place pecans in a brown paper bag and sprinkle in the sugar and cinnamon mixture; shake well.
- ♥ Transfer coated nuts to ungreased cookie sheet; bake for 10 to 20 minutes, or until dry.

MEASURING FRESH & DRIED HERBS

When using dried herbs remember that they are far more concentrated than fresh. Use a fraction of the measurement for fresh herbs, or roughly one third of the amount.

For example, if a recipe calls for 1 Tablespoon of a fresh herb, you will need only 1 teaspoon of dried. (3 teaspoons equal 1 Tablespoon.)

To store fresh rinsed herbs and cut or peeled vegetables, place a damp paper towel in a plastic bag or plastic container. Add herbs or veggies, seal, and store in the refrigerator for up to one week.

Dried herbs should be stored in a cool dry place and checked for potency periodically.

Vegetables

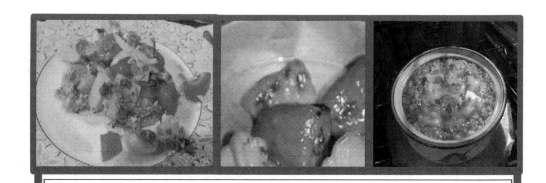

VEGETABLES
Best Dang Onion Rings Ever!
Cherry Tomatoes Élite
Chile Corn Cakes in Banana Peppers
Easter Bunny Pudding
Lake-side Baguettes
Okra & Black Bean Side
Roasted Garlic
Roasted Potatoes & Sweet Garlic
Texas Caviar
The Bomb.com Baked Beans
Verdure al Forno
Whole Wheat Spinach Burritos, Garlic Sauce

Best Dang Onion Rings Ever!

The name says it all. Serve these light and tasty rings with burgers or atop a really great steak. While the batter is made ahead, these onion rings must be fried just before serving to ensure a crispy coating. Serve these to guests who like to help in the kitchen and use an exhaust fan to absorb the smell of frying oil.

Yield: Serves six to eight

12 ounces beer	3 to 4 cups vegetable oil
1½ cups all-purpose flour	1 large yellow onion
½ teaspoon garlic powder	1 large red onion
½ teaspoon kosher salt	Kosher salt

- ♥ Combine beer, flour, garlic powder and salt. Cover; set aside at room temperature for **3 hours**.
- ♥ Ten minutes before preparation, preheat oven to 200 degrees.
- ♥ Peel and cut onions into ¼-inch slices then separate into rings. Line jellyroll pan with paper towels and set aside.
- ♥ In large pot, heat 2 inches of oil to 375 degrees.
- ♥ Using tongs, dip a few onion rings into the batter. Let excess batter drip off; carefully place rings in hot oil. (Do not add too many rings at one time.)
- ♥ Fry rings, turning until lightly browned. Transfer to jellyroll pan, salt lightly, and place in oven to keep warm while other rings are frying. Repeat with remaining rings. Serve immediately.

Cherry Tomatoes Élite

Bring out the flavor of tomatoes by roasting them. This dish is delicious any time of year, but especially good with fresh-picked summer tomatoes and thyme.

Yield: Serves six

1½ pints cherry tomatoes, halved
1½ pints grape tomatoes, halved
1½ Tablespoons, plus ¼ cup, extra virgin olive oil
1 Tablespoon fresh thyme, chopped
1½ teaspoons kosher salt

½ teaspoon freshly ground black pepper
2 large garlic cloves, peeled
2 scallions, minced (including green parts)
1/3 cup fresh parsley, chopped fine
2 cups homemade bread crumbs

- ♥ Preheat oven to 400 degrees.
- ♥ Place tomatoes in a 9 x 13-inch casserole dish. Add 1½ Tablespoons olive oil, thyme, salt and pepper. Toss to mix, and then spread tomatoes evenly in pan.
- ♥ Place garlic, parsley, ½ teaspoon salt in a food processor and process until garlic is chopped fine. Add the bread crumbs and pulse to combine. Add ¼ cup olive oil and pulse to blend.
- ♥ Sprinkle crumbs evenly over tomatoes. Bake for 40 to 45 minutes, or until crumbs are golden and tomatoes juices are bubbling. Serve hot.

Chile Corn Cakes in Banana Peppers

These spicy cakes make a delicious meat-free meal. Serve with a crisp wine for the perfect ending to a summer day.

Yield: Serves six

3 banana peppers
4 Tablespoons extra virgin olive oil
½ red bell pepper, chopped fine
½ yellow bell pepper, chopped fine
4 large ears of fresh raw corn kernels
½ yellow onion, chopped fine
1 Tablespoon chile powder
1 teaspoon ground cumin
¼ cup chicken stock
¾ cup all-purpose flour

1 teaspoon baking powder
½ cup cornmeal
1 large egg, lightly beaten
½ cup skim milk
1 Tablespoon unsalted butter, melted
2 Tablespoons fresh cilantro, chopped
Kosher salt & freshly ground black pepper to taste
Vegetable oil for sautéing

- ♥ Halve banana peppers lengthwise, core and seed. Then lightly roast over an open flame to soften just a bit and bring up the flavor. Remove to a plate and set aside.
- ♥ In a large saucepan over medium-high heat, heat 2 Tablespoons of olive oil and sauté the red peppers, corn and onions for 2 to 3 minutes or until the onions begin to soften. Add the chile powder and cumin and cook for another 2 minutes, stirring constantly.
- ♥ Add the chicken stock and stir, scraping up any flavor-packed browned bits from the bottom of the pan. Continue cooking until most of the liquid has evaporated. Remove from the heat and set aside.
- ♥ Into a small bowl, whisk together the flour and baking powder. Add the cornmeal, egg, milk and butter. Stir until smooth. Add the corn mixture and cilantro. Season to taste with salt and pepper.
- ♥ Stuff Banana pepper "boats" with corn cake mixture, dispersing evenly into six halves.

- ♥ In a large sauté pan over medium-low heat, heat a small amount vegetable oil.
- ♥ Add the peppers stuffed with corn batter and sauté pepper side down until the corn mixtures begins to solidify and peppers begin to brown, 3 to 4 minutes. Carefully flip the stuffed peppers using a long spatula and holding the cake in place as you flip, and cook the batter side. Sauté until the corn cakes are golden brown, 3 to 4 minutes.
- ♥ Remove to paper towels to drain. Cook in batches; add additional oil if necessary. Serve warm with a garnish of sour cream mixed with chopped jalapeño pepper.

Easter Bunny Pudding

This sweet carrot pudding is the perfect accompaniment to an Easter Sunday roast.

Yield: Serves six

2 cups carrots	2½ Tablespoons all-purpose flour
½ cup granulated sugar	½ teaspoon cinnamon
½ cup packed brown sugar	3 large eggs, slightly beaten
¼ cup unsalted butter	1 teaspoon baking powder
1 cup skim milk	½ teaspoon kosher salt

- ♥ Preheat oven to 350 degrees. Cook and purée carrots; measure.
- ♥ In a large bowl, combine all ingredients and mix until well incorporated.
- ♥ Butter a medium-sized casserole dish (approximately 9 x 9-inches), and add mixture. Bake until set, approximately 1½ hours.

Lake-side Baguettes

This large vegetable sandwich is just perfect for a day at the lake. Prepare early in the morning, because the flavors blend as the day wears on and the sandwich just keeps getting better and better. The addition of hard boiled eggs makes this baguette a complete balanced meal. The secret to the delicious filling is in roasting the peppers. This brings out their flavor and softens them just enough to mix well with the other ingredients. Toasting the baguette before stuffing is also essential. The crunchy edges of the baguette remain crisp even after several hours and provide a crisp contrast to the soft vegetable filling.

Yield: Serves six

1 yellow pepper
1 red pepper
½ cup fresh parsley, coarsely chopped
1 15-ounce can large pitted black olives, drained & coarsely chopped
½ pint cherry tomatoes, halved lengthwise
½ bunch scallions, thinly sliced (including green parts)

1 8-ounce jar capers, drained
Freshly ground black pepper & Kosher salt to taste
4 hard-boiled eggs, sliced lengthwise
1½ crusty baguette loaves
½ cup homemade vinaigrette dressing (See recipe with *Hearty Kale Salad*)

- ♥ Roast peppers by broiling them whole over an open flame, as close to heat as possible, until skin is well browned/blackened. Place in a brown paper bag with the top crumpled close until cool enough to handle, about 20 minutes.
- ♥ Peel peppers, leaving some of the charred skin intact; discard rest of skin. Cut peppers in half and seed, then cut into long, thin strips and then into thirds, reserving any liquid; place in a large bowl. Drain and chop olives; halve tomatoes and slice scallions; add. Coarsely chop the parsley and add to peppers along with olives, tomatoes, scallions and capers; Salt and pepper vegetables to taste.

- Add just enough dressing to coat vegetable mixture and stir to combine. Allow vegetables to marinate while you prepare the baguettes.
- Preheat oven to 350 degrees.
- Cut baguettes in half lengthwise. Leaving a "hinge" on one side. Scoop out the middle of loaves. (Save this discarded bread in the freezer to make homemade bread crumbs on another day.) Leave a little bread in place along the edges of each loaf so the filling does not leak out.
- Brush the insides of bread shells gently with dressing and lightly toast in oven for 5 to 7 minutes. Remove from oven, let loaves cool, and then pack marinated vegetables into loaves.
- Place egg slices over vegetables and sprinkle with salt and pepper.
- Close loaves and wrap tightly with plastic wrap and let stand, covered with a cookie sheet weighted with heavy books, for 1 to 3 hours, egg side down. Cut baguettes into 4 to 6 pieces and serve.

PERFECT HARD BOILED EGGS

For hard boiled eggs that turn out tender and delicious each time, follow this simple formula.

1) Place eggs in a saucepan full of cool water, being careful to not overcrowd the pan with too many eggs touching one another.
2) Gently bring the water to a boil, and allow water to boil for just one minute.
3) Remove the pan from the heat and allow eggs to steep, with the lid on tight, for 12 to 15 minutes.
4) Drain, cool and then chill eggs in the refrigerator before peeling.

Okra & Black Bean Side

This is a fresh and low calorie side dish, as well as a great way to enjoy the fruit of a summer garden.

Yield: Serves six

1 Tablespoon olive oil
4 scallions, chopped (including green parts)
2 garlic cloves, minced
1½ cups fresh okra, cubed
1 red bell pepper, chopped
1 jalapeño pepper, seeded & minced

2 large ears fresh raw corn kernels
1 15-ounce can black beans, rinsed & drained
1/3 cup fresh cilantro, minced
Kosher salt &
Freshly ground black pepper

- ♥ Wash and prepare vegetables as directed.
- ♥ Heat oil in a large skillet over medium-high heat. Add onions and garlic; sauté 1 minute. Add okra; sauté 3 minutes.
- ♥ Reduce heat to medium. Add bell and jalapeño peppers; cook 5 minutes. Add corn; cook 5 minutes. Stir in beans; cook 2 minutes.
- ♥ Stir in cilantro; season to taste with salt and pepper.
- ♥ Remove to serving bowl and refrigerate until ready to serve.

Roasted Garlic

Roasted garlic is subtle, sweet, buttery soft and delicious in mashed potatoes, sauces or tossed with hot pasta. Garlic can also be served warm by squeezing cloves from their skins onto crisp crackers or bread. Roasted heads of garlic keep well in the refrigerator, and when roasted whole in the husk, you can easily squeeze out just what you need.

1 (or more) garlic head(s)
Olive oil, good quality

Kosher salt &
Freshly ground black pepper

- ♥ Preheat oven to 350 degrees.
- ♥ Slice off the top ¼-inch of garlic head to reveal the cloves.
- ♥ Drizzle tops with a little (approximately ½ to 1 teaspoon) olive oil and season lightly with salt and pepper. Loosely wrap each individual head in aluminum foil and twist foil together at top to seal.
- ♥ Roast for 25 to 30 minutes, or until the garlic is very soft when squeezed.

OPTIONAL: You can also open the foil for the last ten minutes of baking and allow the garlic to caramelize.

HOW TO MINCE GARLIC

Choose plump, firm heads of garlic that are free of sprouts and dark spots. Garlic will stay fresh for months when stored in a cool, dark place – but not in the refrigerator.

To peel and mince garlic, place the flat side of a large knife on an unpeeled clove. Then gently crush the clove by pressing the knife down with the heel of your hand. Peel off the skin and trim the rough end with your knife.
Mince the clove by cutting lengthwise, then cutting crosswise.

When cooking minced garlic be sure to sauté over low heat and watch carefully. Garlic burns very quickly, which will result in a bitter taste.
If you burn your garlic, discard it and start again.

Roasted Potatoes & Sweet Garlic

Simple yet satisfying, these rustic potatoes are great to serve at dinner parties because they can be prepared ahead, then cooked the final 5 to 10 minutes on high heat to crisp just before the meal is served. The garlic becomes soft and sweet while cooking and the potatoes have a crunchy edge with soft center.

Yield: Serves four

8 large russet potatoes, cubed
6 to 8 Tablespoons unsalted butter
Kosher salt

Freshly ground black pepper
12 cloves garlic

- ♥ Clean and cube potatoes, leaving skin on. Peel garlic and leave whole.
- ♥ Melt butter in a skillet; add potatoes and coat on all sides. Add garlic.
- ♥ Season with salt and pepper to taste. Cover skillet and cook over medium heat for 20 to 25 minutes, tossing occasionally and scraping up crispy pieces. **Remove lid for last 5 to 7 minutes.**

Texas Caviar

Enjoy black-eyed peas on New Year's Day and be assured of good fortune all year! The longer this caviar marinates, the better it gets.

Yield: Serves ten

1 15-ounce can black-eyed peas, rinsed & drained
1 teaspoon vegetable oil
¼ cup warm vinegar
1 teaspoon granulated sugar

1 clove garlic
¼ onion, sliced thin
½ teaspoon kosher salt
Freshly ground black pepper
1 4-ounce can green chilies

- ♥ Chop chilies, then combine all ingredients and mix thoroughly.
- ♥ Store in sealed container in refrigerator for at least two days.
- ♥ Remove garlic clove after one day. Stir often as "caviar" marinates.

SLICING AN ONION

This method not only makes the onion easy to handle, but ensures uniform slices that will cook and/or brown evenly.

Start by halving the onion lengthwise with the grain and notching out the ends. Then hold one half of the onion, flat center side down with your fingertips. Start slicing through to center at bottom edge of one side. Place your knife at a low angle and follow the natural curve of the onion. Adjust the angle of your knife as you slice, keeping it at 90 degrees. Slice until you reach the center, then flip the onion and continue in same manner through opposite side.

If you want to dice your onions, simply continue cutting through these slices in the opposite direction.

The Bomb.com Baked Beans

This recipe for baked beans won Best Runner-up in a Tulsa World cooking contest that I entered in 1998. The combination of beans with beer and sugar make each bite an unexpected burst of flavor. Bring these to a pot luck supper or picnic, but don't expect any to be left over to take home!

Yield: Serves eight to ten

1 32-ounce can great northern beans, drained
1 16-ounce can garbanzo beans, drained
1 16-ounce can pinto beans, drained
½ onion, chopped
1 serrano chile pepper, seeded & minced

½ green pepper, chopped
3 to 4 garlic cloves, minced
½ cup packed brown sugar
2 Tablespoons catsup
½ Tablespoon dijon mustard
6 ounces beer
1 teaspoon tabasco sauce
2 to 4 strips good quality bacon

- ♥ Preheat oven to 350 degrees
- ♥ Combine all ingredients except bacon, then pour into a 9 x 13-inch baking dish.
- ♥ Top beans with bacon and bake approximately 1½ to 2 hours, or until beans are bubbly and bacon is very crisp. Mixture should be thick.

NOTE: When measuring brown sugar, always pack the sugar into the measuring cup or spoon to deflate and ensure an accurate measurement.

Verdure al Forno

Verdure al Forno (vegetables in the oven) is a great one-dish meal that is quick and easy to make. The sweetness of the brown sugar and basil makes a delicious topping when combined with asiago cheese.

Yield: Serves six to eight as a vegetarian entrée, or twelve as a side dish

2 large zucchini
4 carrots
1 large sweet potato
1 yellow onion, sliced thin
½ red pepper, seeded
4 to 5 ounces grape tomatoes, left whole
1 cup homemade bread crumbs
1½ cups asiago cheese, grated

1/3 cup packed brown sugar
4 to 5 fresh basil leaves, minced
¼ cup fresh parsley, minced
2 large garlic cloves, minced
3 teaspoons kosher salt
½ teaspoon freshly ground black pepper
½ cup butter, cut into ¼-inch cubes
2 teaspoons olive oil

- ♥ Preheat oven to 350 degrees.
- ♥ Quarter and slice zucchini, carrots, sweet potatoes and red peppers into uniform ½-inch cubes. Grease a 9 x 13-inch casserole dish and add prepared vegetables.
- ♥ Mix bread crumbs, cheese, brown sugar, herbs, garlic, salt and pepper and sprinkle evenly over vegetables. Dot with butter cubes and lightly drizzle with olive oil.
- ♥ Bake for 1½ hours, or until carrots have softened and topping is browned and bubbly.

Whole-Wheat Spinach Burritos

This healthy family meal can be prepared in just one half hour from start to finish and is popular with kids. These yummy "vegetarian" burritos are especially good served with homemade Salsa Fresca (See recipe in Appetizers*) and Garlic Sauce (See recipe below).*

Yield: Six burritos

1 pound fresh spinach
2 cloves garlic, minced
1 teaspoon freshly ground black pepper

½ teaspoon ground cumin
6 whole-wheat tortillas
8 ounces cheddar cheese, grated

- ♥ Preheat oven to 375 degrees.
- ♥ Wash and chop spinach; steam 1 to 2 minutes and blot any moisture from leaves with paper towels. Add garlic, pepper and cumin; mix well. Spoon spinach mixture evenly into each tortilla and top with cheese. Roll into burritos and place in greased 9 x 12-inch baking pan.
- ♥ Sprinkle additional cheese on top. Bake for 15 to 20 minutes, or until cheese is bubbly and tortillas are crispy on top.
- ♥ While burritos are baking, prepare salsa, garlic sauce and some black beans. Serve hot.

Garlic Sauce

This is a tasty alternative to plain-old sour cream. Yield: About one cup.

1 cup light sour cream
2 Tablespoons extra virgin olive oil
4 garlic cloves, minced

¼ teaspoon kosher salt
Freshly ground black pepper

- ♥ In a small bowl, whisk together sour cream and olive oil until blended.
- ♥ Mash the garlic and salt together until the mixture forms a paste. Stir the garlic paste into the sour cream. Season with pepper to taste.
- ♥ Cover and refrigerate until ready to use.

EASY HOMEMADE BREAD CRUMBS

Fresh bread crumbs always enhance your recipes. Here's an easy way to make them at home.

For one cup of bread crumbs, toast two slices of whole wheat bread until very crisp. Lightly butter toast and sprinkle a small amount of salt and garlic powder on top. Tear bread into a food processor and pulse into crumbs.

42

Pasta, Eggs, Dressing & Sauce

PASTA & EGGS

Comfort Risotto with Asparagus & Lemon
Fettuccini with Green Beans & Walnuts
Homemade Pizza with Tomato Sauce
Rustic lasagna, Sausage & Three Cheeses
Emily's Egg Bake

DRESSING & SAUCE

Bleu Cheese Dressing
Easy Apple Butter
Fool-Proof Hollandaise Sauce

Comfort Risotto with Asparagus & Lemon

Creamy rice with bites of mushroom and asparagus seasoned with fresh lemon is truly delicious comfort food. This is also a great dish to prepare when you have a kitchen helper. One of you can stir the risotto, while the other prepares the rest of the ingredients, enjoying each other's company in the process. Fresh tender asparagus is a must for this dish as it is added at the last minute and just barely cooked.

Yield: Serves six

4 Tablespoons unsalted butter
1 shallot, minced
1½ cups arborio rice
1 large portobello mushroom
1½ Tablespoons roasted garlic (See recipe in *Vegetable* section)
½ cup crisp white wine
5 to 6 cups chicken broth

¼ cup fresh parmesan cheese, grated
2 teaspoons rind of lemon, grated
1 cup asparagus
¼ cup fresh chives, minced
Kosher salt & freshly ground black pepper to taste
Additional parmesan cheese & Chives for garnish

- ♥ Cube mushroom into ¼ to ½-inch pieces; break off woody stems and slice asparagus on the diagonal into ½-inch pieces; prepare other vegetables and herbs.
- ♥ Melt 3 Tablespoons of butter in a medium saucepan and sauté the shallots over medium heat until soft but not brown. Add the rice and mushrooms and sauté evenly until the rice is translucent, about 3 minutes. Add the garlic, wine, and ½ cup of the broth and cook, stirring constantly, until the liquid is absorbed. Continue adding small amounts of broth and cooking in this manner until the rice is creamy but the center is firm, about 15 minutes.
- ♥ When the risotto is done, stir in the remaining 1 Tablespoon of butter, grated cheese, lemon rind, asparagus and chives, and season with salt and pepper. Serve in warm bowls garnished with chives cut into 1-inch lengths and shaved parmesan cheese.

ROASTING ASPARAGUS ON THE GRILL

*Asparagus roasted on the grill has a delicious smoky flavor
with a hint of olive oil.*

Simply wash asparagus and break off the woody parts.
*Asparagus spears will snap naturally between the woody bottom and soft edible
stalks and flowery tops.*

Use a 10-inch piece of heavy-duty aluminum foil to create a throw-away pan.
Fold the 4 edges of foil over about ½-inch, twice, to make a sturdy border, like a
jelly roll pan. Place asparagus into your "pan" and drizzle lightly with olive oil,
then sprinkle with kosher salt and freshly ground black pepper.
Place pan of asparagus on a hot grill and roast for 4 to 5 minutes until
crisp yet tender.
Turn stalks and redistribute the bubbling oil as you go.

Fettuccine with Green Beans & Walnuts

I love pasta with nuts. This is made even more delightful with the addition of fresh green beans.

Yield: Serves four

½ cup walnuts	Kosher salt &
3 Tablespoons unsalted butter	Freshly ground black pepper
3 shallots, chopped fine	1 pound fresh green beans
¾ cup fresh basil leaves, julienned	¾ pound fettuccine pasta
3 large garlic cloves, minced	Rind of 1 lemon, grated
1 cup chicken broth	Fresh parmesan cheese, grated
1 cup crème frâiche	4 whole basil leaves

- ♥ Toast walnuts in 350 degree oven for 5 to 7 minutes; cool and chop.
- ♥ Melt butter in large saucepan and add shallots, cooking over medium heat for 1 minute. Add 2 Tablespoons basil, garlic and broth.
- ♥ Cook over medium heat until shallots are softened. Stir in crème fraiche and cook until slightly thickened. Season with salt and pepper to taste.
- ♥ In the meantime, cook pasta and steam green beans.
- ♥ Serve on 4 individual plates topping pasta with green beans then coating with sauce. Sprinkle nuts on top.

GARNISH: Grated lemon rind, whole basil leaves, grated parmesan cheese.

Homemade Pizza

I began making homemade pizza when my sons were about ten. They got a kick out of helping punch down the dough and add the toppings to the pies. Homemade pizza night was always popular, and a fun treat for both our sons and their friends. We have very fond memories of sitting around the table with half a dozen young guys laughing and telling stories over this homespun meal. It's worth every minute spent in the kitchen when you see how much it is enjoyed. Spend a Saturday or Sunday afternoon preparing this special treat for dinner with family and friends. Be sure to allow a good 3 to 4 hours to prepare.

Yield: Two medium-large sized pizzas

BASIC PIZZA DOUGH

Start your pizza dough around noon in order to serve for dinner.

4½ cups all-purpose flour	2 teaspoons granulated sugar
1 envelope active dry yeast	1¾ cups very warm water
2 Tablespoons extra virgin olive oil	Additional flour
1 teaspoon kosher salt	

- ♥ Prepare dough in a Kitchen Aid, or heavy duty mixer and start with mixing hook attached. Place 4½ cups flour in mixing bowl and make a well in the center with your hand.
- ♥ Mix yeast, oil, salt and sugar in warm water (110-115 degrees), then add to center of the well. Mix on speed one until blended. With the dough hook attachment and mixer on speed two, knead dough for 5 minutes. Remove dough from bowl and dust with flour, then place in a bowl greased with olive oil.
- ♥ Cover the bowl with a kitchen towel and let rise in a warm spot until double in bulk, approximately 1½ hours. Punch down the dough and knead briefly with your hands, then divide into two equal parts and shape into balls. Set balls in a warm spot and let rise again, approximately 20 minutes.
- ♥ Oil a pizza brick (recommended) or cookie sheet, as well as hands, and roll and stretch each ball to cover the entire brick/sheet, leaving a lip on the outer edge all around. (Use flour to adhere the lip in place.)

BEST PIZZA SAUCE

While dough is rising, prepare your sauce and toppings.

2 Tablespoons olive oil

1 medium red onion, chopped

2 cloves garlic, minced

1 28-ounce can Italian plum tomatoes (or 2 pounds fresh tomatoes)

1 8-ounce can tomato sauce

2 Tablespoons fresh basil, chopped

½ teaspoon kosher salt

¼ teaspoon freshly ground black pepper

1 bay leaf

- ♥ Sauté onion in olive oil in a large pot until transparent; add garlic and sauté another minute. Add tomatoes, sauce, ½ of the basil, salt, pepper and bay leaf and bring to a boil. Reduce heat and simmer uncovered for about 45 minutes, until thickened, stirring occasionally.
- ♥ Add the remaining basil and cook another 15 minutes.
- ♥ Remove bay leaf before spreading sauce evenly onto uncooked pizzas, spread onto bricks/sheets.

TOPPINGS

These are my favorite toppings.

1 to 1½-pounds sweet Italian sausage

1 green bell pepper, sliced thin

1 red bell pepper, sliced thin

1 pound mushrooms, sliced thin

½ red onion, sliced thin

1 Tablespoon olive oil

½ teaspoon kosher salt

¼ teaspoon freshly ground black pepper

6 to 8 fresh basil leaves, julienned

1 15-ounce can large pitted black olives, chopped

1 pound mozzarella cheese, grated

½ pound fresh parmesan cheese, grated

- ♥ Preheat oven to 500 degrees.
- ♥ Brown and crumble sausage and set aside. Prepare vegetables; chop olives into chunks.
- ♥ Sauté green and red peppers, mushrooms, onion in olive oil until just soft and still crisp; season with salt and pepper.

- ♥ Divide all ingredients evenly over two pizzas (covered with sauce). Sprinkle pies with fresh basil leaves and black olives. Sprinkle on mozzarella cheese and parmesan cheese.
- ♥ Bake in a hot oven for 20 to 30 minutes, or until center of pies are bubbling and crusts are golden brown. (Be sure the center is bubbly or the dough will be undercooked.)

ॐ _____ ॐ

Rustic Lasagna with Sausage & Three-Cheeses

This rustic lasagna is loaded with cheese and sprinkled with sausage. The pasta is only cooked a few minutes before assembly and then cooks through while in the poaching liquid, making it really savory and flavorful.

Yield: Serves six

½ pound lasagna noodles
3 Tablespoons extra-virgin olive oil, plus more for tossing
½ pound sweet Italian sausage
1 cup water
6 large cloves garlic, sliced thin
1 28-ounce can whole tomatoes, chopped with juices reserved

Kosher salt &
Freshly ground black pepper
4 ounces fresh parmesan cheese, grated
½ pound mozzarella cheese
4 ounces Italian fontina cheese
¼ cup fresh basil leaves, julienned

- ♥ Preheat oven to 425 degrees.

- In a large pot of boiling salted water, cook the lasagna noodles al dente, or about 5 minutes. Drain and transfer the noodles to a bowl of cold water and let stand for 2 minutes, then drain well. Transfer noodles to another bowl and toss with a bit of olive oil to prevent sticking.
- In a medium skillet, heat 1 Tablespoon of the olive oil. Add the sausage, cover and cook over medium heat, turning/stirring, until browned all over. Crumble sausage as it cooks. Add the water, cover and simmer until the sausage is just cooked through, about 4 minutes.
- In a large skillet, heat the remaining 2 Tablespoons of olive oil. Add the garlic and cook over low heat until golden, about 3 minutes. Add the tomatoes with their juices and cook over medium heat for 10 minutes, stirring occasionally.
- Slice mozzarella and fontina cheese into 8 thin pieces.
- Transfer the sausage to a plate; add the sausage poaching liquid to tomatoes and simmer for 4 minutes. Simmer the sauce over medium heat until thickened, about 12 minutes.
- Season the sauce with salt and pepper. In a well-buttered, 9 x 13-inch baking dish, arrange 3 lasagna noodles. Spoon about ¼ cup of the tomato sauce over each lasagna noodle and sprinkle with a little grated parmesan cheese. Set a piece of the mozzarella and fontina on each lasagna noodle and add a few spoonfuls of sausage. Repeat the process two more times with the remaining lasagna noodles, tomato sauce, mozzarella, fontina and sausage, sprinkling with a little more parmesan.
- Bake the lasagna on the top rack of the oven for 20 minutes, until the sauce starts to bubble. Raise the oven temperature to 450 degrees and bake for 7 minutes longer, until the top is richly browned. Let the lasagna rest for about 10 minutes, then scatter the sliced basil on top, cut into squares and serve.

NOTE: Lasagna takes about 1½ hours to prepare; 1 hour to assemble and ½ hour to bake. It's just as easy to make two lasagnas as only one, so I typically double this recipe, allowing one lasagna to freeze and enjoy later. Unbaked lasagna can be refrigerated overnight and baked just before serving, or frozen, thawed and baked.

Emily's Egg Bake

My pretty daughter-in-law Emily is a wonderful cook and gracious hostess. It is fun to watch her with Robby in the kitchen. They are a symphony of coordinated movements and harmony! On Christmas morning, the first time our family enjoyed the holiday together in their Colorado home, Emily treated us to these delicious eggs — a buttery bake with a chile kick.

Yield: Serves six to eight

10 large eggs
½ cup all-purpose flour
1 teaspoon baking powder
1 teaspoon salt

1 pint cottage cheese
1 pound cheddar cheese
1/2 cup butter, melted
2 8-ounce cans green chilies, diced

- ♥ Preheat oven to 350 degrees.
- ♥ Beat eggs. Whisk flour, baking powder and salt together; add to eggs.
- ♥ Add cheeses, butter and chilies.
- ♥ Bake in a 9 x 13-inch casserole dish for 35 minutes, or until browned and bubbly.

Bleu Cheese Dressing

This classic dressing is scrumptious over a fresh chilled wedge of ice berg lettuce with a sprinkling of sliced red onion, cherry tomatoes and grilled shrimp on the side.

Yields: Two and one-half cups

1 cup sour cream
¾ cup mayonnaise
½ teaspoon dry mustard
1 teaspoon kosher salt

½ teaspoon freshly ground black pepper
2 teaspoons worcestershire sauce
4 ounces bleu cheese, crumbled

- ♥ Whisk together first six ingredients.
- ♥ Add crumbled bleu cheese and stir until combined.
- ♥ Refrigerate 24 hours before serving.

NOTE: Use good quality mayonnaise, such as Hellman's.

❧ _____ ☙

Easy Apple Butter

This apple butter is made in a crock pot and takes just a few minutes to assemble. Apple butter is delicious on biscuits, muffins or toast.

Yield: Two pints

3 pounds apples
½ cup granulated sugar
½ cup packed brown sugar
½ Tablespoon maple syrup
½ Tablespoon ground cinnamon
¼ teaspoon nutmeg

¼ teaspoon ground cloves
1 teaspoon salt
½ Tablespoon pure vanilla extract

53

- ♥ Peel, core and cube apples; place in a crock pot.
- ♥ Mix all remaining ingredients except extract and pour over the apples; combine. Cook on low setting for **10 hours**, stirring occasionally, until mixture is thick and dark brown.
- ♥ Stir in vanilla and continue cooking for **2 more hours**.
- ♥ In a food processor, puree apples until smooth and buttery; Spoon into sterile jars.

NOTE: Apple Butter will keep in the refrigerator for up to two weeks. It also freezes well.

C   ɛ

Fool-Proof Hollandaise Sauce

This is a fool-proof recipe for a sauce that can be intimidating to make.

Yield: Serves six

3 large egg yolks
Juice of ½ fresh lemon
Kosher salt

Freshly ground black pepper
½ cup butter, melted

- ♥ In a blender or food processor, combine yolks, lemon, salt and pepper, and mix thoroughly.
- ♥ Melt butter in sauce pan. Once butter is melted and hot, *slowly* drizzle into egg mixture as blender is running. (The egg yolks will cook as the butter is added.) Blend another 1 to 2 minutes after all butter has been incorporated to thicken sauce.
- ♥ Serve immediately. This sauce does not re-heat or keep well.

Poultry
& Fish

POULTRY

Chicken Divan with Rye & Cayenne

Comfort Chicken Pot Pie

"Healthy" Fried Chicken

Officer's Wives Chicken Salad

Roast Chicken with Currants & Pistachio Rice

Secret Roast Turkey & Scrumptious Pan Gravy

Southwest Avocado Chicken

Weeknight Chicken with Garlic & Tomatoes

FISH

Asparagus & Crab-Corn Fritters, Saffron Sauce

Grilled Chipotle Shrimp

Grilled Salmon & Corn Salsa with Basil Cream

Pink on Green: Salmon with Spinach Pasta

Chicken Divan with Rye & Cayenne

This Chicken Divan has a hint of rye and a white sauce laced with cayenne pepper.

Yield: Serves six

WHITE SAUCE

½ cup shallots, minced
½ teaspoon curry powder
2 Tablespoon unsalted butter
4 Tablespoons all-purpose flour
3 cups skim milk

1½ cups chicken broth
2 egg yolks, lightly beaten
Juice of 1 fresh lemon
Kosher salt
½ teaspoon cayenne pepper

- ♥ Sauté shallots and curry in butter in a saucepan over medium heat.
- ♥ Add flour; cook for 1 minute to make a paste. Whisk in milk and broth to turn paste into a sauce; simmer over medium-high heat until thickened, about 5 minutes, whisking often.
- ♥ Whisk some of the hot sauce into the egg yolk to temper. Then stir yolk mixture back into sauce. Reduce heat to low, and cook sauce for 1 minute, stirring constantly to avoid lumps.
- ♥ Remove from heat and stir in lemon juice, salt and cayenne.

NOTE: When preparing the sauce, be careful to not add the egg yolk directly to the hot sauce or it will scramble. Temper the yolk by first whisking some of the hot milk mixture into it. Then it can be added to the rest of the white sauce, stirring over low heat to thicken.

FILLING

3 cups mushrooms, halved
Kosher salt &
Freshly ground black pepper
2 Tablespoons butter

2 slices rye bread
2 cups rotisserie chicken
2 cups fresh broccoli florets
6 ounces asiago cheese, grated

- ♥ Preheat oven to 375 degrees.

- ♥ Sauté mushrooms, broccoli and seasonings in butter in medium skillet over medium heat until browned.
- ♥ Tear chicken into 1-inch pieces. Toast bread and cut into cubes. Add toasted bread, chicken, broccoli and mushrooms to an 8 x 8-inch casserole dish. Pour the sauce over; top with cheese.

TOPPING

4 slices rye bread

- ♥ Toast and lightly butter bread. Process toasted rye bread in food processor until crumbled. Sprinkle crumbs over casserole.
- ♥ Place casserole on baking sheet and bake for 35 to 40 minutes, or until brown and bubbly.

℘_____℘

Comfort Chicken Pot Pie

This is real comfort food. My mother's pie crust and a rich white sauce are balanced with green peas, tiny pearl onions and carrots.

Yield: One pie, serves six

WHITE SAUCE

6 Tablespoons unsalted butter
6 Tablespoons all-purpose flour
2 cups chicken broth

1 cup skim milk
1 teaspoon kosher salt
½ teaspoon ground black pepper

- ♥ Melt butter in a saucepan; stir flour into butter. Cook, whisking for 2 minutes, or until the mixture begins to solidify. Slowly add the broth, whisking until smooth and well combined. Slowly add the milk, whisking until smooth and well combined. Season with salt and pepper. Cook for 5 minutes, until thickened and smooth.

CHICKEN & VEGETABLES

4 large chicken breasts	1 heaping cup fresh or frozen carrot coins
½ onion	
2 bay leaves	1 heaping cup fresh or frozen peas
	½ cup fresh or frozen pearl onions
	1 teaspoon kosher salt

- ♥ Bring 4 chicken breasts, ½ onion and 2 bay leaves to a boil in salted water. Then reduce heat and simmer for approximately **20 to 30 minutes**, or until chicken is cooked. Remove chicken, allow to cool enough to handle, and tear into bite-sized pieces, removing any fat and grizzle as you go. Discard poaching liquid.
- ♥ In the meantime, if using fresh vegetables, wash and pat dry. Cut carrots into coins and parboil to soften just a bit.

PIE CRUST

I/3 recipe Gladdie's Pie Crust (See recipe with *Pies*)

- ♥ Preheat oven to 400 degrees.
- ♥ Roll two rounds of pie crust, one for bottom of pie and one for the top.
- ♥ Place one round of prepared pie crust in pie plate, allowing enough overhang so that the edges can be crimped; chill.
- ♥ In a large bowl, combine chicken pieces and vegetables and season with salt; pour in white sauce and stir gently to coat chicken and vegetables with sauce.
- ♥ Pour chicken mixture into chilled pie shell and add three small dollops of butter to top. Cut vents in the second crust to allow the steam to escape; place on top of filled pie; fold and crimp edges to seal. Sprinkle top of pie with kosher salt.
- ♥ Bake for 20 minutes at 400 degrees, then reduce heat to 375 degrees and cook for another 40 minutes, or until center of pie is bubbly and crust is golden brown. Protect crust with pie shield during the first 40 minutes of baking.

"Healthy" Fried Chicken

This time-honored dish is made just a bit healthier by pre-steaming the chicken and removing the skin. Steaming guarantees a moist chicken and reduces the time the chicken spends frying, also making it less greasy.

Yield: Serves four

2 pounds skinless chicken (breasts, thighs and legs)
1 large egg
1 cup buttermilk
½ cup all-purpose flour

1 teaspoon kosher salt
½ teaspoon freshly ground black pepper
1½ quarts vegetable oil

- ♥ In a large kettle, bring 2 inches of water to a boil.
- ♥ Set the chicken on a grate over the water. Cover the kettle and steam the chicken until it is almost cooked, approximately 15 to 18 minutes, turning at half-way point. Remove the chicken from steam and cool.
- ♥ In a medium bowl whisk the egg and buttermilk together. In a separate bowl, combine the flour, salt and pepper. Marinate the chicken in buttermilk mixture for 5 minutes, then remove and dredge in seasoned flour.
- ♥ In a large skillet, heat oil to 365 degrees. Fry the chicken in batches for approximately 7 minutes per side, or until golden brown.
- ♥ Remove chicken to paper towels to drain, and serve immediately while hot and crispy.

Officer's Wives Chicken Salad

This recipe is from my mother-in-law, who spent many years as an officer's wife in the U.S. Air Force. While the men were away on missions, she and the other women on base supported and comforted one another sharing friendship and good food. This salad was a popular choice. I often make this salad for my own support system. My girlfriends enjoy the water chestnuts that provide a crunch to every bite, and the lemon juice that makes the dressing light and fresh.

Yield: Serves six to eight

1 small whole roasted chicken
2 ounces almonds
1 cup light mayonnaise
½ teaspoon curry powder
1 Tablespoon soy sauce
1 cup celery, sliced

1½ 6-ounce cans water chestnuts, drained & sliced
1 pound seedless grapes, halved lengthwise
1 Tablespoon fresh lemon juice

- ♥ Remove meat from the chicken and tear into bites-sized pieces; transfer to large mixing bowl. Toast almonds 10 minutes at 350 degrees; allow to cool before chopping. Mix mayonnaise, curry, and soy sauce.
- ♥ Combine celery, water chestnuts, grapes and lemon juice. Add to mayonnaise mixture.
- ♥ Add celery and mayonnaise mixture to chicken. Chill salad 1 to 2 hours.
- ♥ Serve over a bed of fresh lettuce and sprinkle almonds on top at last minute to ensure they retain their crunch.

NOTE: Whole roasted chickens can be purchased fully cooked in most grocery stores.

Roast Chicken with Currants & Pistachio Rice

This chicken is a great choice when entertaining friends. It is easy to make ahead, leaving only a fresh vegetable to prepare once guests arrive. The currants provide a sweet surprise and the pistachios bring an unexpected crunch to the savory roast and sweet rice.

Yield: Serves four to six

1 4-pound roasting chicken
Juice of 1 lemon (reserve half)
Kosher salt
8 Tablespoons unsalted butter (divided)
½ yellow onion, minced
½ cup currants, plumped

½ cup pistachios, chopped
½ teaspoon ground turmeric
½ teaspoon ground cumin
2 cups rice, cooked
Kosher salt & freshly ground black pepper to taste

- ♥ Preheat oven to 375 degrees.
- ♥ Plump currants in ½ cup of brandy for 20 to 30 minutes, or until soft and supple. Cook rice per package instructions. Hull and chop nuts. Rinse chicken and blot dry.
- ♥ Pour half of lemon juice inside cavity; salt lightly.
- ♥ In small skillet, melt 4 Tablespoons butter and sauté onion over low heat until golden. Add currants, pistachios, turmeric and cumin.
- ♥ Combine onion mixture with rice; mix well. Add salt and pepper.
- ♥ Stuff chicken with rice mixture; truss. Put in roasting pan; sprinkle lightly with salt and pepper. Combine reserved lemon juice and remaining butter (melted); spread over chicken breast.
- ♥ Roast 1½ hours, basting occasionally.

Secret Roast Turkey

This is a no-fail formula for a perfectly moist turkey that's seasoned to the bone.
The secret is in the brining. *Two good things happen in this process. Salt draws out the*
blood, cleansing the bird, and is absorbed in the meat - which becomes juicy and seasoned
right down to the bone. Second, the sugar rounds out the salty flavor and helps the turkey
brown. If you have purchased a frozen turkey, brining will greatly improve the flavor.
This method can also be used to roast a chicken.

Yield: Serves ten to twelve

BRINING THE BIRD

You'll need to brine your turkey for 10 to 12 hours before roasting it.
Don't worry if a small portion of the turkey is not submerged in the brine.

In a large stockpot or plastic tub, mix 1½ gallons of water with 1½ cups salt and 1
cup sugar; stir to dissolve. Add the turkey to the brine, breast side down, and
refrigerate for 10 to 12 hours, covered.
Remove the turkey from the brine, rinse it in cold water and pat dry with paper
towels. Discard the brine.

1½ cups kosher salt
1 cup granulated sugar
1 12 to 14-pound turkey
2 medium onions, coarsely chopped

2 carrots, coarsely chopped
2 celery ribs, coarsely chopped
Fresh parsley, sage, rosemary &
thyme
3 Tablespoons unsalted butter,
melted

- ♥ Preheat the oven to 400 degrees.
- ♥ Remove neck, wing tips, giblets and cavity fat from bird.
- ♥ Tie herbs into a small bouquet. Prepare vegetables.
- ♥ Place half of the onions, carrots, celery and the herbs in the turkey cavity.
- ♥ Using kitchen string tie the turkey legs together. Then bring the string
  around the turkey and tie the wings at the breast.

- ♥ Scatter the remaining onions, carrots and celery in a large roasting pan. Oil a V-shaped rack and set it in the pan. Transfer the turkey to the rack, breast side up. Brush the turkey with melted butter.
- ♥ Pour 1 cup of water into the pan and roast the turkey for **45 minutes**.
- ♥ Baste the turkey with the pan juices and add 1 more cup of water to the pan. Roast the turkey for about 1 hour and 45 minutes longer, basting it with the pan juices every 30 minutes or so and adding another ½ cup of water to the roasting pan whenever the vegetables begin to brown. *(To ensure juicy breast meat, rotate the turkey a quarter turn each time you baste it.)*
- ♥ **The turkey is done when an instant-read thermometer inserted in an inner thigh registers 170 degrees.**
- ♥ Transfer the turkey to a carving board, tent (cover loosely with foil) and let rest for 20 to 30 minutes to ensure juices are retained in the meat before carving.
- ♥ Reserve the juices in the roasting pan for making the gravy (See recipe on following page).

NOTE: The turkey can be prepared through removal from the brine and refrigerated for up to 8 hours before roasting. The gravy can be made ahead through the first step and then held.

Choose a small, fresh turkey in the 14-pound & under category.

Large turkeys take longer to cook, making the outer meat likely to overcook and dry out before the interior meat is cooked. If you are feeding more than 12 people, buy two small turkeys rather than one big one.

When serving two small turkeys, cook the first one early in the day. Carve it, arrange it on an ovenproof platter and cover it with foil. Meanwhile, roast the second turkey. Just before serving, set the platter in a 350 degree oven to warm the meat. Use the whole bird for show and pass the carved turkey. Carve the second turkey once everyone has had a first serving.

DRESSING: Cook the dressing in an ovenproof dish, not inside the turkey. A stuffed bird takes longer to cook through than an unstuffed one. The longer the turkey sits in a hot oven, the more it overcooks and dries out.

CARVING: When carving your turkey, remove both wings first. Separate each wing from the body at the joint. Remove each leg and set aside. Remove each breast half from the bone in one piece, then thinly slice each half crosswise. Cut each leg at the joint, and then carve the meat from the thigh and drumstick.

Scrumptious Pan Gravy

Yield: About one quart

2 teaspoons vegetable oil
1 medium onion, chopped
4½ cups water
Reserved pan juices from turkey

1 cup dry white wine
3 Tablespoons cornstarch
Freshly ground black pepper

- ♥ Heat the oil in a large saucepan. Add onion and cook over medium high heat until lightly browned, about 5 minutes. Cover and cook over low heat about 20 minutes. Add 4 cups of the water and bring to a boil. Cover partially and simmer over low heat until the broth is reduced to 3 cups, about **1 hour**. Strain the broth into a medium saucepan and skim off the fat.
- ♥ Pour the reserved turkey pan juices into a glass measuring cup and skim off the fat. Set the roasting pan over two burners on medium high heat. Add the wine and boil for 2 minutes, scraping up the flavorful brown bits from the bottom of the pan. Scape the contents of the pan into a strainer set over the turkey broth and press on the roasted vegetables. Bring the broth to a boil.
- ♥ Mix the cornstarch with the remaining ½ cup of water until smooth, and then whisk this slurry into the boiling broth. Reduce the heat to low and simmer until lightly thickened, about 2 minutes.
- ♥ Season with pepper, pour into a gravy boat and serve immediately.

Southwest Avocado Chicken

This spicy chicken can be prepared in just a few minutes. I made this on many a night when our boys were busy with school and sports.

Yield: Serves four

4 skinless chicken breasts
1 teaspoon ground cumin
½ teaspoon kosher salt
¼ teaspoon freshly ground black pepper
1 Tablespoon olive oil

2 cloves garlic, minced
1 cup Salsa Fresca (See recipe in *Appetizers*)
1/3 cup light sour cream
1 ripe avocado
Fresh cilantro, chopped

- ♥ Sprinkle chicken with cumin, salt and pepper. Heat oil in 10-inch skillet over medium high heat.
- ♥ Cook chicken and garlic in oil until lightly browned; about 2 minutes per side. Add salsa; cover and simmer until chicken is tender; about 10 minutes. Remove chicken to serving platter; keep warm. Peel, seed and slice avocado.
- ♥ Stir sour cream into skillet juices until well blended. Spoon over chicken; top with avocado slices. Serve immediately with extra salsa on the side.

GARNISH: Chopped cilantro

HOW TO PREPARE AVOCADOS

Avocados add a mild, nutty flavor and buttery texture to your dishes, and are easy to prepare using this method.

♥ Start with a large knife. Insert it into the top of fruit where the stem was, and gently press down until you reach the pit.
♥ Holding the knife steady, rotate the fruit so that the knife traverses the pit, cutting the entire avocado in two.
♥ Remove the knife, and then gently twist the two sides away from one another with your hands to separate.
♥ Strike the pit with your knife, and pierce it with the blade. Twist and remove the knife; the pit will come out with it.
♥ Then, use the knife's tip to slice the flesh in both horizontal and vertical rows, being careful not to cut through the skin. Remove the meat from fruit by gently scooping it out with a spoon. Your avocado will spill out already diced and ready to use!
♥ Be sure to quickly squeeze fresh lemon juice on the diced fruit to prevent browning.

Weeknight Chicken with Garlic & Tomatoes

This recipe is quick, easy and delicious. The garlic becomes sweet and mild when cooked slowly, and the fresh sage just makes the dish.

Yield: Serves four to six

3 Tablespoons olive oil
4 large skinless chicken breasts
1 15-ounce can stewed tomatoes
10 large garlic cloves
¼ cup white wine

6 to 8 fresh sage leaves, left whole
Kosher salt & freshly ground black pepper
Fresh parmesan cheese, grated

- ♥ Heat olive oil in a large skillet over medium heat.
- ♥ Peel garlic and leave cloves whole. Season chicken with salt and pepper and cook about 2 minutes on each side, or until golden brown. Lower heat; add tomatoes, garlic, wine and sage. Cover and simmer 15 minutes. Mash tomatoes lightly with a fork to make a sauce.
- ♥ Serve with white beans or mashed potatoes and a fresh green vegetable.
- ♥ Top with grated parmesan cheese while hot.

Asparagus Salad with Crab-Corn Fritters & Saffron Sauce

The arugula provides just enough tartness to balance the incredibly creamy sauce, and the asparagus and cheese fill out the meal. Seasonal corn is essential to these fritters. The fritters can be kept hot in a 300-degree oven while the salad is prepared. Then assemble all on one plate and serve with crispy bread.

Yield: Serves four to six

SALAD

Arugula lettuce mix
1 bunch fresh asparagus

4 to 6 wedges soft creamy cheese, such as havarti or Swiss

- ♥ Preheat oven to 400 degrees.
- ♥ Clean asparagus by removing woody parts and stems, place on a baking sheet and brush lightly with olive oil, kosher salt and freshly ground black pepper, and roast for 5 to 8 minutes.
- ♥ Cut cheese into 1 x 1½-inch triangular-shaped wedges, one for each serving.

Corn Fritters

8 Tablespoons unsalted butter
5 scallions, chopped (including green parts)
3 large ears fresh raw corn kernels
12 ounces fresh crab meat
1 cup all-purpose flour

1 teaspoon baking powder
1 teaspoon paprika
¾ teaspoon Old Bay seasoning
1 teaspoon kosher salt
2 large eggs, beaten lightly
½ cup skim milk

- ♥ Remove corn kernels from cob. Parboil crab 8 to 10 minutes; cool and tear into bite-sized pieces.
- ♥ Melt 2 Tablespoons butter in medium pan over medium heat. Add scallions and corn and sauté for 3 minutes, until soft. Add crab and cook an additional minute. Set aside.

- ♥ Mix flour with baking powder, paprika, Old Bay and salt in large bowl. Then make a well in the center of flour mixture and whisk in eggs and milk, stirring until the mixture is smooth with the consistency of a pancake batter. Stir in the corn and crab mixture.
- ♥ Heat 2 to 3 Tablespoons butter in large skillet over medium-high heat.
- ♥ For each fritter, drop 2 rounded Tablespoons of the batter into the hot butter and cook for 2 to 3 minutes on each side, or until golden brown and firm. Be careful to not overcrowd your skillet to ensure fritters brown evenly on all sides. Repeat process as necessary until all batter is used, adding additional butter if necessary.

NOTE: The batter for fritters can be made up to an hour ahead of cooking time and refrigerated.

Saffron & Chile Sauce

3 large garlic cloves, minced
½ teaspoon saffron threads
2 teaspoons Sriracha chile sauce
Juice of ½ fresh lemon
¾ cup mayonnaise

½ teaspoon kosher salt
¼ teaspoon freshly ground black pepper
½ cup parsley, minced

- ♥ Place garlic, saffron, chili sauce, lemon juice, mayonnaise, salt and pepper in food processor and purée until smooth. Fold in parsley.

ASSEMBLY:
- ♥ Divide lettuce onto serving plates and place one wedge of cheese onto each bed. Divide asparagus evenly and place onto each plate atop lettuce. Add 2 fritters to each plate and top with two generous dollops of sauce.

HOW TO SHUCK CORN

When purchasing fresh corn, check for natural moisture. The husks should not appear dry, and when pulled back, the kernels should be plump, tight, and vivid yellow (or bright white) in color.

To shuck fresh corn, hold the tip facing down and pull the husks and silk toward your body. Use a damp paper towel and your hands to remove any remaining silks by twisting back and forth on the ear.
Trim about a half-inch from the top of each ear before cooking.

To trim the kernels from the cob, stand ears upright in a pie plate.
Use a sharp knife from top to bottom in a slow, sawing motion.
Remove kernels in rows.

DEVEINING SHRIMP

Always shop for the freshest shrimp you can find and peel and devein them yourself.
Peeling is easy; it's the deveining that takes time.
But the vein is the waste from the shrimp, so you want to do the job well.

Once shrimp are peeled, run a small paring knife along the top back of the shrimp. You will find a dark, slimy vein as you cut just below the surface. Use the tip of your knife to scrape this out. Be sure to run your knife the full length of the shrimp. Once the vein has been completely removed, rinse shrimp in cool water then prepare to cook.

Grilled Chipotle Shrimp

This spicy shrimp is both succulent and smoky because it is marinated and then glazed while grilling.

Yield: Serves four to six

2 Tablespoons olive oil
½ onion, finely chopped
5 cloves garlic, minced
2 teaspoons ground cumin
1 Tablespoon fresh oregano, minced
Kosher salt &
Freshly ground black pepper to taste

1 chipotle chile in adobo sauce
¼ cup wine vinegar
1 cup water
1½ pounds large shrimp
1 Tablespoon packed brown sugar
¼ cup orange juice, freshly squeezed
1 Tablespoons adobo sauce (from canned chilies)

MARINADE

♥ Peel and devein shrimp. Heat the olive oil in a medium-sized skillet over medium-high heat; add onions and sauté until golden brown (approximately 10 minutes).

♥ Add the garlic, cumin, oregano, salt and pepper and cook another minute. Put mixture into a food processor; add chipotle chilies, vinegar and water; purée. Pour half of the purée into a glass or plastic bowl and allow to cool. Add the shrimp to the cooled mixture and allow to marinate for **1 to 2 hours** in the refrigerator.

GLAZE

♥ Pour the remaining purée into a medium saucepan; add the brown sugar, orange juice and adobo sauce. Over a medium-high heat, bring to a boil; reduce heat and simmer until slightly thickened, approximately 10 minutes. Remove from heat; set aside.

GRILLING

♥ Preheat grill. Remove shrimp from the marinade and thread on skewers; brush with glaze. Grill 2 to 3 minutes per side, until shrimp turns pink. Frequently brush shrimp while grilling with additional glaze. Remove from heat and serve immediately.

Grilled Salmon & Corn Salsa with Basil Cream

This is a light summery dish that takes advantage of fresh corn and a good cut of salmon.

Yield: Serves four

SALMON

1/3 cup good quality olive oil
2 teaspoons rind of lemon, grated
½ teaspoon kosher salt
¼ teaspoon freshly ground black pepper

4 6-ounce salmon fillets, ½-inch thick
Basil Cream (See recipe below)
Roasted Corn Salsa (See recipe on following page)

- ♥ In a mixing bowl, whisk together the olive oil, lemon rind, salt, and pepper. Rub the salmon with the marinade and marinate in refrigerator for **1 hour**.
- ♥ Make the Warm Basil Cream; Have the salsa ready.
- ♥ Grill salmon on a moderately hot grill for 15 to 20 minutes.
  Leave the skin on salmon while grilling, as it will help fillet hold together and not flake and fall through the cracks while grilling. Peel skin from fillet before serving.

GARNISH: Chopped cilantro.

Basil Cream

1 Tablespoon olive oil
2 shallots, chopped
6 cloves garlic, minced
½ cup crisp white wine
2 cups chicken broth
½ teaspoon fennel seed
1 cup half and half cream

4 cups lightly packed basil leaves
1 Tablespoon parsley, chopped
Kosher salt &
Freshly ground black pepper
Fresh lemon juice
1 plum tomato, diced

- ♥ Crush fennel seed in mortar and pestle to release flavor.
- ♥ In a saucepan, heat the olive oil and sauté shallots and garlic until soft and brown. Add wine, stock and fennel seed; bring to a boil. Then lower the heat and reduce by half. Add the cream and reduce to a light sauce consistency. Remove to a food processor.
- ♥ Blanch the basil leaves quickly in lightly salted boiling water. Drain and run cold water over them immediately to stop the cooking and set the color. Pat dry. Add the blanched basil leaves and the chopped parsley to the cream mixture in the processor and process until smooth. Return the contents to a saucepan and season with salt, pepper, and a few drops of lemon juice.
- ♥ At serving time, stir in the tomatoes and serve immediately.

Corn Salsa

4 large ears fresh raw corn kernels
¼ cup olive oil
Kosher salt & freshly ground black pepper to taste
½ red bell pepper, diced
½ yellow onion, diced

1/3 cup fresh basil, chopped
½ serrano chili, seeded & minced
3 Tablespoons rice wine vinegar
1 teaspoon fresh lemon juice
1 teaspoon honey

- ♥ Preheat oven to 425 degrees. Remove corn kernels from cobs.
- ♥ Toss the corn kernels with olive oil and lightly season with salt and pepper. Spread out the kernels in a single layer on a baking sheet and roast until very lightly browned, about 15 minutes. Set aside.
- ♥ In a separate bowl, combine the remaining ingredients.
- ♥ Stir in roasted corn. Season with additional salt and pepper, lemon juice and honey. Cover and store refrigerated for up to 5 days.

NOTE: This roasted salsa can be made ahead, but the basil cream does not keep – make it while the salmon marinates.

SEEDING & ROASTING CHILE PEPPERS

Just as hot chilies can set your taste buds on fire, they can also burn your hands if not prepared properly. Serrano and jalapeño peppers add wonderful depth to recipes via a chemical called capsaicin that will also burn your skin. Control the capsaicin "kick" by removing the seeds and veins, but be sure to wear surgical or rubber gloves when you do!

Seed peppers by using a paring knife to cut off the stem, and then slice lengthwise. Cut each half lengthwise to create four separate pieces. Lay the skin side down on a cutting board and slide your knife against the pepper to cut away the vein and seeds.

Wash your hands while still in the gloves with warm soapy water – then remove the gloves, thus ensuring that none of the capsaicin touches your skin. If your hands tingle, rub some aloe gel or lotion on them. And, if you eat something too spicy, don't reach for water or an alcoholic beverage! This will intensify the heat and the liquid will spread the capsaicin throughout your mouth – yikes! Eat a bite of cheese or sour cream or drink some milk instead. This will cool the burn.

Seeding & Roasting chilies helps remove the bitter taste of their skin and brings out the earthy flavor. The easiest way to roast is over a gas burner. You can also roast on the grill or under an oven broiler. The objective is to blister and blacken the skin without damaging the flesh of the chile. Once this has been accomplished, place the chile in a plastic or paper bag. The steam in the enclosed bag will loosen the skin so it can be easily removed. Do not run roasted chilies under water because this will remove the essential oils and smoky taste. After skinning, cut the chile open and remove the ribs, seeds and core. Roasted chilies can be stored in the refrigerator for up to 2 days, or frozen for 6 months.

When buying chilies, choose those that are flexible and without blemishes. If you do not plan to use them immediately, prevent drying out by storing them in the freezer. Soak dried peppers in hot water for about 30 minutes to reconstitute.

Pink on Green:
Salmon with Spinach Pasta

Pink on Green is not only delicious, but a really pretty dish. The salmon steeps in the delicious wine sauce making it moist and flavorful. The nutmeg and dill both complement and contrast each other and are perfect with the cream. Be sure to use fresh linguine pasta and herbs.

Yield: Serves four

½ **pound fresh salmon fillet**
2 **cups dry white wine**
6 **sprigs parsley, chopped**
6 **whole black peppercorns**
2 **cups half and half cream**
¼ **teaspoon nutmeg**

4 **Tablespoons unsalted butter, melted**
1 **teaspoon kosher salt**
1 **pound spinach linguine**
2 **to 3 Tablespoons fresh parmesan cheese, grated**
½ **cup fresh dill, chopped**

- ♥ Poach salmon in wine, parsley and peppercorns for 10 minutes.
- ♥ Cool, and then flake salmon with fork, removing skin and bones.
- ♥ Simmer half and half, nutmeg, salt and 2 Tablespoons butter in saucepan until cream is reduced by one-third.
- ♥ Cook linguine al dente in boiling salted water, approximately 3 to 5 minutes. While pasta is cooking, stir parmesan cheese, salmon and ¼ cup fresh dill into cream mixture.
- ♥ Toss drained linguine with remaining 2 Tablespoons butter and divide pasta onto plates. Spoon salmon cream sauce over linguine.

GARNISH: Remaining fresh dill.

Beef

BEEF

GB2: Gorgonzola Burgers for Growing Boys
Indiana Spaghetti & Meatballs
Marinated Flank Steak
Mountain Top Boeuf Bourguignon
Polpettone with Tomato Sauce
Pot Roast to Happiness
Prime Rib in Rock Salt
Stuffed Bell Peppers

GB2:

Gorgonzola Burgers for Growing Boys

We have so many good memories of preparing these burgers for our sons and their friends. The bacon flavors the burger while it grills and helps hold in the juices. Great for growing boys!

Yield: Serves six

2 pounds ground chuck
Kosher salt &
Freshly ground black pepper
6 strips good quality, smoked
bacon
6 to 12 slices gorgonzola cheese

6 kaiser rolls
Leaf lettuce (enough for six
sandwiches)
2 beef steak tomatoes, sliced thick
¼ red onion, sliced paper thin

- ♥ Preheat grill. Prepare lettuce, tomato and onion.
- ♥ Make ground chuck into 6 hamburger patties. Wrap each patty with a strip or two of bacon and secure with toothpicks; season with salt and pepper on both sides.
- ♥ Grill burgers on a hot grill to desired doneness, turning only once (See *Grilling a Great Burger* on following page).
- ♥ Once burgers are flipped, top with gorgonzola cheese so that it can melt while second side of burger cooks.
- ♥ Split and butter rolls. Toast rolls, butter side down during last few minutes of grilling.
- ♥ Serve with lettuce, tomato, onion.

OPTIONAL: Ground chuck can be substituted with Bison.

HOW TO GRILL A GREAT BURGER

Buy the right meat.
For juicy burgers, get ground chuck with a fat content of 15 to 18 percent.
Lean and extra-lean meat make tough, dry burgers.
The more freshly ground the meat is, the more tender and flavorful the burger.
If your store has a butcher, ask them to grind the meat
fresh for you.

♥ **Use as few pats as possible to form patties.** The more you handle the meat, the tougher your burger will be. Once patties are made, lightly salt and pepper both sides.

♥ **Use a clean, oiled, preheated grill.** Bits of debris on your grill will cause your meat to stick to the grate, as does an unoiled surface and too low a temperature. *(A neat way to oil the grill is to use a small bundle of fresh rosemary as your brush.)*

♥ **Flip burgers once and at the right time.** Constant turning will toughen and dry out meat, and if you flip burgers too soon, they will stick.

♥ **Cook :**

RARE	2 minutes per side
MEDIUM-RARE	3 minutes per side
MEDIUM	4 minutes per side
WELL-DONE	5 minutes per side

♥ **Don't press on the burgers while they're cooking.** You don't want to lose the juice that seeps out as it holds most of the flavor.

Indiana Spaghetti & Meat Balls

In north central Indiana where I grew up, there is a large contingency of Italian Americans. This is a sampling of their authentic cooking. The sauce is sweet and savory and the meatballs are nothing short of excellent. Both the meat balls and sauce freeze well.

Yield: Serves twelve

MEATBALLS

4 large eggs
1 cup skim milk
4 to 6 slices (depending on size) coarse wheat bread
1¼ pounds lean ground beef
¾ pound Italian sausage

1 medium yellow onion, chopped fine
1 cup fresh parsley, minced
4 cloves garlic, minced
2 teaspoons kosher salt
½ teaspoon freshly ground black pepper

- ♥ Preheat oven to 450 degrees.
- ♥ Toast then crumble bread fine in food processor. Beat eggs slightly in medium sized bowl. Add milk and bread crumbs; mix well. Let stand for five minutes.
- ♥ Add beef, sausage, onions, parsley, garlic, salt and pepper; mix until well combined. Shape into 48 to 60 meatballs, 1 to 1½- inch in diameter. Place in two 9x13-inch greased baking pans. Bake uncovered for **30 minutes,** or until golden brown and cooked through.

SAUCE

½ cup good quality olive oil
1 medium yellow onion, chopped
4 cloves garlic, minced
3 Tablespoons granulated sugar
1½ Tablespoons kosher salt
¼ cup fresh basil, chopped fine

1½ cups water
1 teaspoon fennel seed
½ teaspoon freshly ground black pepper
2 28-ounce cans whole tomatoes
1 6-ounce cans tomato paste

- ♥ Crush fennel seed with mortar and pestle to release flavor. Heat oil in large Dutch oven over medium heat. Add onion and garlic; sauté until golden. Add sugar, salt, basil, fennel, pepper, tomatoes, paste and water. Bring to a boil; reduce heat and simmer, covered for **30 minutes**.
- ♥ Add meatballs and drippings. **Simmer covered for 1 hour,** stirring occasionally.

TO SERVE

2 pounds spaghetti

1 cup fresh parmesan cheese, shaved
Fresh parsley

- ♥ Cook spaghetti per instructions below, drain and rinse in cold water.
- ♥ Place on serving dish and top with meatballs and sauce.
- ♥ Sprinkle with shaved cheese and parsley sprigs.

PERFECT PASTA EVERY TIME

Although fresh pasta is always preferable, a great formula for cooking dried pasta is as follows:

Use a large pasta pot filled with salted water. Bring water to a rolling boil and then add pasta. Ensure all pasta is submerged and then stir to divide each strand. *Boil pasta for 15 minutes.* Drain and rinse briefly in cool water to remove the sticky paste and stop the cooking.

For fresh pasta, reduce boiling time to just 3 to 5 minutes.

To "hold" cooked and drained pasta and ensure it is supple when ready to serve, simply dip it back into a pot of simmering water for a few seconds to rehydrate just before plating.

Marinated Flank Steak

This steak makes an elegant meal when served with roasted potatoes and a fresh vegetable. The marinade acts as a tenderizer, and the honey caramelizes as the meat grills, giving this steak a wonderful, slightly crispy surface with a juicy and tender interior. My husband serves this steak as a sandwich to his friends. After slicing the beef diagonally, he cuts each slice into two-inch pieces, and then serves in warm rolls for a yummy slider.

Yield: Serves six

2½ **pounds flank steak**
¼ **cup soy sauce**
2 **Tablespoons honey**
½ **cup vegetable oil**
2 **Tablespoons vinegar**

1½ **teaspoons garlic powder**
1½ **teaspoons ground ginger**
2 **scallions, chopped (including green parts)**

- ♥ Combine soy sauce, honey, oil, vinegar, garlic powder, ginger and green onions. Place steak in flat casserole. Pour sauce over; cover and **marinate overnight**.
- ♥ Place on *hot* grill and pour half of the remaining marinade on top to encourage flaming and charring. Pour second half of marinade over steak after flipping. Cook to desired doneness, flipping only once, approximately 4 to 6 minutes on each side for medium rare.
- ♥ Slice ½-inch thick across grain on diagonal.

NOTE: *Flank steak must be tenderized.* Marinate for a minimum of 12 hours. Overnight is preferable.

Mountain Top Boeuf Bourguignon

From first bite to last slurp, this French bistro-style bourguignon satisfies. My husband and I first enjoyed this in the Swiss Alps while staying in the 100-year old **Hotel Obersteinberg atop Mount Tschingelshorn***. Accompanied by mashed potatoes, crusty brown bread and a salad of beets topped with diced white onion picked from the mountain top garden, we were sure we'd never tasted anything more delicious. Afterwards we were provided only a candle by which to see, and slept like babies under a blanket of down in a dormitory bunkhouse that had no electricity.*

Yield: Serves six

4 bone-in short ribs (2 inches thick, 2 pounds total)	4 shallots, minced
Kosher salt &	4 celery stalks, coarsely chopped
Freshly ground black pepper	2 strips bacon
2 teaspoons cornstarch	1 Tablespoon tomato paste
3 Tablespoons extra virgin olive oil	4 fresh thyme sprigs
12 ounces white button mushrooms, quartered	1 dried bay leaf
5 carrots	1½ cups dry red wine
	6 cups beef broth
	1 cup water

- ♥ Season ribs with salt and pepper. Coat with cornstarch.
- ♥ Heat oil in a large heavy pot over medium-high heat. Lightly brown ribs on all sides, about 6 minutes. Transfer to a plate.
- ♥ Prepare vegetables; finely chop 3 carrots and cut remaining 2 into ¾-inch cubes. Slice bacon crosswise into thin strips.
- ♥ Add mushrooms to pot. Cook until browned, about 4 minutes. Transfer to a bowl with cubed carrots and reserve.

- ♥ Add shallots, finely chopped carrots, celery, and bacon to pot. Cook until caramelized, about 6 minutes. Stir in tomato paste.
- ♥ Return ribs with plate juices to pot. Add thyme and bay leaf. Raise heat to high. Add wine. Cook, scraping up flavorful brown bits with a wooden spoon, until slightly reduced, about 1 minute.
- ♥ Add stock and water. Bring to a boil. Reduce heat, and simmer, partially covered, until beef is tender, **2 to 2½ hours**.
- ♥ Remove ribs. Separate meat from bones; discard bones. Cut meat into bite-size pieces; return to pot. Add reserved mushroom-carrot mixture. Bring to a simmer; cook until carrots are tender. Season with salt.

NOTE: This dish can be refrigerated for up to 2 days or frozen for up to 1 month. Thaw before using. Skim fat from top, and reheat.

Polpettone with Tomato Sauce

This stuffed meat loaf recipe originated in Naples Italy and is one of my favorites. It exemplifies simple yet classic southern Italian cuisine. This recipe makes two loaves and a double recipe of sauce. Both the Polpettone and Tomato Sauce freeze well.

Yield: Serves twelve

POLPETTONE

¾ pound lean ground beef

¾ pound Italian sausage

1 cup bread crumbs (homemade are best)

2 large eggs, beaten lightly

2 Tablespoons fresh parmesan cheese, grated

2 cloves garlic, minced

2 Tablespoons parsley, minced

Kosher salt &

Freshly ground black pepper

½ pound mozzarella cheese, sliced

- ♥ Preheat oven to 350 degrees.
- ♥ Mix all ingredients, excluding mozzarella, in a large bowl until well combined. Divide mixture into four equal parts. Flatten two parts into two loaf baking pans. Reserve remaining two parts.
- ♥ On each of the bottom parts, place the sliced mozzarella. Cover with the top parts, sealing all sides so that the cheese will not seep out while baking. Bake for 1 hour.
- ♥ Serve with fresh pasta and top with tomato sauce (See recipe below).

BASIC TOMATO SAUCE

This tomato sauce is also excellent for lasagna, manicotti and other pastas.

5 to 6 Tablespoons good quality olive oil

½ onion, diced

4 cloves garlic, minced

1 6-ounce can tomato paste

6 ounces water

3 8-ounce cans tomatoes

Kosher salt &

Freshly ground black pepper

6 fresh basil leaves, chopped

♥   Heat oil in a medium sauce pan. Sauté onion and garlic until golden brown. Add tomato paste and stir, adding one can of water to reduce thickness. Simmer for 15 minutes. Mix in tomatoes, salt, pepper and basil. **Simmer for 1 hour**.

CAUTION WHEN USING BAY LEAVES
THEY CANNOT BE DIGESTED!

It is important to always remember to remove bay leaves after they have simmered in your recipes. The leaves are too course for the human stomach to process and can tear your intestines.

Pot Roast to Happiness

This pot roast makes my husband so happy! It is also the best pot roast I've ever tasted. The mushroom soup and moisture from the combination of vegetables creates a light and delicious broth. On a Sunday afternoon, put this in to roast at noon, your home will smell delicious all day, and a complete meal will be ready by 6:00 pm.

Yield: Serves six

1 3 to 4-pound chuck roast	3 Tablespoons worcestershire sauce
1 pound fresh carrots	½ teaspoon garlic powder
6 boiling onions	1 10½-ounce can condensed cream
1 green pepper	of mushroom soup
2 stalks celery	Kosher salt & freshly ground black
6 small baking potatoes	pepper to taste

- ♥ Preheat oven to 300 degrees. Prepare vegetables: Chop carrots into 3 to 4-inch lengths; remove stems from onions and leave whole; remove seeds from pepper and cube; cut celery into 2 to 3-inch lengths; quarter potatoes leaving skin on.
- ♥ Place roast into a large roasting pan and season with worcestershire sauce, garlic powder, salt and pepper. Place vegetables around perimeter of roast and season with salt and pepper. Coat the top of roast with mushroom soup. Cover and bake for 5 to 6 hours.
- ♥ During the last hour, baste beef and vegetables with the soup broth, and gently rotate vegetables to ensure even browning.

Prime Rib in Rock Salt

*Prime rib cooked under a blanket of rock salt keeps the meat tender, with an end result that isn't too salty. Prime Rib in Rock Salt has been a Christmas Eve staple with the Alfrey family for many years. **My Dad John** took great care in choosing only the best aged beef, always meeting with the Butcher in person.*

Yield: Serves eight

1 4 to 6-pound prime rib of beef roast
2 Tablespoons worcestershire sauce
2 teaspoons garlic powder
2 to 3 Tablespoons freshly ground black pepper

3 4-pound packages rock salt
½ cup water
Disposable aluminum foil roasting pan

- ♥ Preheat oven to 500 degrees.
- ♥ Brush roast with worcestershire sauce; sprinkle with garlic powder. Rub pepper an all sides of roast.
- ♥ Pour half of the rock salt into a large bowl and mix with a small amount of water, stirring to make salt slightly pasty.
- ♥ Pour the remaining rock salt to depth of ½-inch in disposable aluminum foil roasting pan; place roast in center of pan. (Salt clings to pan, so be sure to use a disposable one.)
- ♥ Add pasty rock salt, covering roast and patting with your hands to seal the roast on all sides. Roast for 12 minutes per pound, or until meat thermometer registers 150 degrees (medium rare) or to desired degree of doneness.
- ♥ Crack salt with hammer; remove roast, and brush away rock salt.

NOTE: Roast continues to cook after taken from the oven. Do not rely on a thermometer alone, but the formula of 12 minutes per pound for medium rare.

Stuffed Bell Peppers

These peppers are a hearty dish on a cold winter's night. The banana peppers provide the shazamm!

Yield: Serves six

½ pound lean ground beef
½ pound ground sausage
6 large green or red bell peppers
1¼ cups long grain white rice
¼ medium sweet onion, diced
2 large garlic cloves, minced
1 8-ounce can tomatoes, diced with their juices

1 8-ounce can Rotel tomatoes & green chilies
2 plum tomatoes, diced
1 banana pepper, diced
8 ounces sharp cheddar cheese, grated
1 to 2 teaspoons kosher salt
Freshly ground black pepper

- ♥ Preheat oven to 400 degrees
- ♥ Cut top from bell peppers, remove seeds and ribs. Place in glass baking dish lightly coated with cooking spray.
- ♥ In a medium sauce pan, cook rice according to package directions.
- ♥ In a large skillet, brown the ground beef and sausage with onion and garlic. Drain the meat. Add the tomatoes and banana pepper to beef mixture. Simmer 5 to 10 minutes. Remove from heat.
- ♥ Stir in cooked rice and season with salt and pepper.
- ♥ Stuff bell peppers with mixture, dividing evenly. Cover the baking dish with aluminum foil and bake for 40 minutes to steam the peppers and mingle the flavors.
- ♥ Remove foil and top each pepper with a generous and even amount of grated cheese. Return to the oven for 5 to 10 minutes, until cheese melts and begins to brown.

NOTE: Stuffed peppers can be frozen whole. When ready to use, just thaw and bake, then top with cheese per instructions above.

Breads, Sweets & Ice Cream

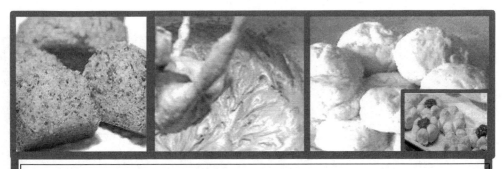

BREADS

Alfrey Rolls

Crunchy Corn Biscuits

Grandma Alfrey's Banana Nut Bread

Lemon Nut Bread

Michael's Pumpkin & Chocolate Muffins

Three-Way Buttermilk Biscuits

SWEETS & ICE CREAM

Betty's Bourbon Sauce

Coco's Cocoa Frosting

Fresh Fruit Crisp

Fourth of July Ice Cream

Mama's Ice Cream Sandwiches

Alfrey Rolls

My mother was beloved for these rolls. They are fluffy and buttery, and can be made plain as dinner rolls, or rolled with cinnamon and sugar. As a child I woke every Thanksgiving morning to the aroma of yeast and cinnamon with our kitchen counters covered with pans and pans of rising rolls for the family gathering later that day. Monroe, a second cousin in Peru Indiana carries on the tradition of baking these rolls back home. **My son Robby** *makes the Colorado rolls, and I make the rolls in Oklahoma. Thanks Mom!*

Yield: Two dozen rolls or two rings

> *Be sure to note this recipe calls for mashed potatoes.*
> *Mom used to make extra mashed potatoes for our dinner the night before she planned to make rolls. Having the potatoes ready saves time in preparation.*

2 large eggs, beaten
1 cup milk
½ cup granulated sugar
1 cup unsalted butter

1 cup mashed potatoes
2 envelopes active dry yeast
1½ teaspoons salt
5 cups all-purpose flour

- ♥ Scald milk; stirring frequently to prevent a film from forming. As soon as the milk bubbles, remove from heat. Add butter, salt, sugar and potatoes. Beat eggs and add.
- ♥ Soften yeast in ¼ cup warm (110 to 115 degrees) water.
- ♥ Add softened yeast to milk mixture, checking to ensure the milk temperature is also not above 115 degrees before adding. If necessary, allow the milk to cool to appropriate temperature before continuing.

- ♥ Transfer to an electric mixer. Gradually add 5 cups of flour that has been sifted with the salt, beating well after each addition.
- ♥ Cover mixing bowl with a kitchen towel and place in a warm spot in your kitchen. Let dough rise to top of bowl.
- ♥ Gently punch risen dough down into the bowl, cover, and let rise again.
- ♥ Make dough into dinner rolls (See instructions below) or cinnamon rolls, or rings, and let dough rise a third time.
- ♥ Preheat oven to 400 degrees.
- ♥ Bake for about 15 minutes, or until golden brown.
- ♥ Bake rings 20 to 25 minutes at 375 degrees.
- ♥ Lightly brush dinner rolls with butter while they are still warm (optional).
- ♥ Cool and ice cinnamon rolls and rings with powdered sugar icing (See recipe on following page).

CAUTION WHEN USING YEAST

Be careful to not scald your yeast.

Water must be lukewarm, 110 to 115 degrees, not hot. Use a candy thermometer to check temperature and allow water to cool if it is too hot.
Rolls will not rise if yeast has been overheated.

DINNER ROLLS

- ♥ Divide dough in half and roll on floured countertop into two large circles about ½-inch thick. Using a round cookie cutter or rim of a glass, cut out discs and place on greased cookie sheet.
- ♥ After placing discs on cookie sheet, fold one side over to meet opposite side of disc, and press the center of outer rim down with your finger tip to adhere in place. Use a dot of melted butter between pressed dough to act as "glue." Re-roll dough as needed until all has been made into discs. Let rise. Bake as directed above.

CINNAMON ROLLS

- ♥ Divide dough in half and roll on floured countertop into two oblong shapes about ½-inch thick. Spread shapes evenly with melted butter. (About ½ cup for two shapes.) Mix sugar with fresh ground cinnamon and sprinkle onto melted butter liberally.

- ♥ Carefully roll shapes into a log, capturing the butter and sugar mixture inside as you roll. Slice logs into about ¾-inch rolls and place on cookie sheet. Let rise. Bake as directed.

CINNAMON RINGS

- ♥ Prepare as logs as per steps for cinnamon rolls above.
- ♥ Rather than cutting rolled log shapes into individual rolls, shape logs into a circle. Press ends of log together to adhere into a ring. Let rise.
- ♥ Gently slice vents in top layer of dough every 2 to 3-inches before baking as directed.

Icing for Cinnamon Rolls & Rings

1 1-pound box powdered sugar　　　**1½ teaspoons pure vanilla extract**
¼ cup butter, softened　　　**2 Tablespoons milk**

- ♥ Mix butter with sugar. Add vanilla.
- ♥ Gradually add milk until reaching desired consistency. Whisk until light and creamy, adjusting the amount of milk as necessary to ensure icing is both thin and creamy. Lightly drizzle icing over rolls or rings.

NOTE: A 1-pound box of powdered sugar is equal to 4 cups.

Crunchy Corn Biscuits

These crunchy biscuits are a great alternative to corn bread. They are very quick and easy to prepare. You can also mix the batter and roll out ahead, and then just bake when your meal is nearly ready to serve.

Yield: One dozen two-inch biscuits or twenty-four miniature biscuits

1 8½-ounce can creamed yellow corn
2 cups Bisquick mix

½ cup unsalted butter
2 Tablespoons fresh chives, minced

- ♥ Preheat oven to 450 degrees.
- ♥ Stir corn and Bisquick together. Add chives and fold gently to combine.
- ♥ Roll out dough on a lightly floured surface to ½-inch thickness. Cut into 2-inch rounds.
- ♥ Melt butter in an oblong casserole dish. Dip rounds into butter and coat on both sides. Return to pan, lining up three across and four down. Bake until golden, about 10 minutes.

Grandma Alfrey's Banana Nut Bread

My grandmother Nellie Alfrey *was raised on a cotton plantation in Hope Arkansas where they served true Southern cooking. This is her recipe. I like to enjoy a buttered slice of this bread right out of the oven while the bread is still warm and the top is crunchy!*

Yield: Two small loaves or one large loaf

2 cups granulated sugar
½ cup unsalted butter, softened
2 large eggs, slightly beaten
3 cups all-purpose flour
½ teaspoon salt

1½ teaspoons soda in
½ cup buttermilk
3 to 4 ripe bananas, well beaten
¼ cup black walnuts, chopped

- ♥ Preheat oven to 300 degrees.
- ♥ Beat sugar and butter until fluffy; add eggs and mix well.
- ♥ Sift flour with salt; add to egg and sugar mixture.
- ♥ Mix soda with buttermilk; add to mixture. Stir in bananas and nuts.
- ♥ Turn batter into greased and floured loaf pan(s).
- ♥ Bake for 1 hour. Slice and serve warm, topped with butter.

OPTIONAL: Add 1 teaspoon rind of orange, grated, to batter before turning into pan(s).

Lemon Nut Bread

A syrupy glaze soaks into this bread after baking, and the fresh lemon juice gives this sweet nut bread a delicious tang.

Yield: One loaf

BREAD

1½ cups all-purpose flour
½ teaspoon salt
1 teaspoon baking powder
½ cup unsalted butter, softened
1 cup granulated sugar

2 large eggs, slightly beaten
½ cup skim milk
½ cup pecans, chopped
Rind of 1 lemon, grated

- ♥ Preheat oven to 350 degrees.
- ♥ Whisk flour, salt and baking powder together; set aside. Cream butter and sugar. Beat in eggs.
- ♥ Add dry ingredients to butter mixture alternately with milk. Beat until smooth. Fold in pecans and lemon rind. Pour batter into a greased loaf pan. Bake for 45 to 50 minutes or until a toothpick inserted into center of loaf comes out clean.

GLAZE

¼ cup sugar

Juice of 1 fresh lemon

- ♥ Combine sugar and lemon juice.
- ♥ Prick hot loaf with toothpick across entire top surface, inserting the full length of the toothpick into the bread. Pour on glaze; let stand for 15 to 20 minutes.
- ♥ Remove from pan and allow to cool completely before slicing.

OPTIONAL: Fold one cup fresh blueberries, coated with one Tablespoon of flour, into batter after incorporating the nuts and rind. Bake in a Bundt pan for 45 to 55 minutes. Glaze as directed, using a long skewer rather than a toothpick to pierce the cake.

Michael's Pumpkin & Chocolate Muffins

These muffins are a must when fall rolls around.
My son Michael *especially loves this moist pumpkin bread studded with chocolate chips.*

Yield: Two dozen muffins

3 1/3 cups all-purpose flour
2 cups granulated sugar
2 teaspoons pumpkin pie spice
2 teaspoons cinnamon
2 teaspoons baking soda

½ teaspoon baking powder
½ teaspoon salt
4 large eggs
1 15-ounce can pure pumpkin
1 cup unsalted butter, melted
2 cups Ghirardelli milk chocolate chips

- ♥ Preheat oven to 350 degrees.
- ♥ In a large bowl with electric mixer, mix dry ingredients until well combined.
- ♥ Beat together eggs, pumpkin and butter. Pour over dry ingredients and mix until just moistened. Fold in chocolate chips.
- ♥ Spoon batter evenly into muffin tins with paper liners.
- ♥ Bake for 18 to 20 minutes, or until toothpick inserted into center of muffin comes out clean.

NOTE: Be sure to use pure pumpkin, not pumpkin pie filling.

Three-Way Buttermilk Biscuits

These biscuits are light and crusty on the outside and moist on the inside. They are also versatile and can be made three ways.

Yield: Sixteen to eighteen biscuits

Buttermilk Biscuits

2 cups all-purpose flour
½ teaspoon salt
2 teaspoons baking powder
½ teaspoon cream of tartar
½ teaspoon baking soda

1 Tablespoon granulated sugar
½ cup Crisco vegetable shortening, cubed
2/3 cup cold buttermilk

- ♥ Preheat oven to 425 degrees. Grease cookie sheet.
- ♥ Whisk dry ingredients (flour, salt, baking powder, cream of tartar, soda and sugar) together in a large bowl.
- ♥ Add shortening and cut into the flour mixture with a pastry blender until the mixture resembles coarse meal. Add the buttermilk all at once and stir just until the dough forms a ball around the fork.
- ♥ Turn dough onto a clean and lightly floured countertop and knead slightly, folding over to encourage flaking. Then roll into a large round ½-inch thick. Cut round with a 2-inch diameter cookie cutter until all dough has been used, taking care to handle dough as little as possible.
- ♥ Place biscuits, touching each other, on the cookie sheet and bake for 15 to 20 minutes until golden.

NOTE: Buy Crisco shortening in bars. They are much easier to use and avoid the messy process involved when measuring into cups.

Cheddar Chive Biscuits

1 recipe Buttermilk Biscuits   ½ cup fresh chives, minced
4 ounces cheddar cheese, cubed

- ♥ Prepare biscuit dough as directed on previous page.
- ♥ Cut cheese into ¼-inch cubes; mince chives.
- ♥ Before rolling out, add cheese and chives and fold gently until well combined. Roll out and bake as directed on opposite page.

Daisy Biscuits

1 recipe Buttermilk Biscuits   Favorite jam

- ♥ Prepare Buttermilk Biscuits as directed through placement on cookie sheet.
- ♥ Make 6 slits through uncooked biscuit dough rounds around edges to ¼-inch from the center. With the end of a wooden spoon handle, make a depression in the center of each biscuit.
- ♥ Spoon ½ teaspoon jam into each biscuit indentation. Bake as directed.

BISCUITS & FRIED APPLES

Biscuits and fried apples are real home cookin'.
The sugary syrup from apples fried in butter melts into the flaky buttermilk biscuits. This is a wonderful treat on New Year's day – or any weekend morning.

4 to 5 apples (per each biscuit recipe) cored and sliced thin.
½+ cup granulated sugar
2 to 4 Tablespoons butter

In a large skillet, fry apples slices in butter until soft but slightly crunchy and the sugar begins to caramelize. Add sugar to taste (depending on the sweetness of your apples) while cooking.
Butter biscuits lightly, top with fried apples, *and go to heaven* – yum!

Betty's Bourbon Sauce

My mother-in-law Betty *serves this sauce over her famous Minced Meat Pie at Christmas time. The sauce is also delicious over bread pudding, or scooped up with your finger tip one luscious taste at a time!*

Yield: Enough sauce to accompany one pie

¼ cup unsalted butter
1 cup granulated sugar
1 Tablespoon cornstarch
1 cup half and half cream

1 teaspoon pure vanilla extract
1/3 cup good bourbon, such as
Maker's Mark

- ♥ Mix sugar and cornstarch in a bowl; set aside.
- ♥ In a saucepan, melt butter then add sugar mixture and stir until dissolved.
- ♥ Slowly add the cream and cook until thickened slightly. Remove from heat.
- ♥ Stir in the bourbon. Serve warm.

NOTE: This sauce keeps well in the refrigerator, and can be made ahead and re-heated in the microwave when ready to serve.

Coco's Cocoa Frosting

Godiva chocolate liqueur makes this frosting exceptional… Delicious on vanilla cupcakes!

Yield: Enough icing for one two-layer cake or twenty-four cup cakes

3 Tablespoons unsalted butter, softened
¼ cup Ghirardelli sweet ground chocolate & cocoa

2 1/3 cups powdered sugar, sifted
2 Tablespoons skim milk
1½ teaspoons Godiva liqueur

- ♥ In a bowl with electric mixer at medium speed, cream butter with cocoa until thoroughly combined and crumbly (approximately 3 minutes).
- ♥ Add the sifted powdered sugar and beat (another 2 to 3 minutes).
- ♥ Add the milk and liqueur and whip until light and fluffy (another 3 to 5 minutes).

Fresh Fruit Crisp

This comforting dessert is chewy and delicious. The secret ingredient is the parmesan cheese. Be sure to use old fashioned rolled oats, not instant, and whatever fresh fruits are in season. I like blackberries in June, peaches in August and apples in the fall!

Yield: Serves eight to ten

6 cups fresh fruit
1½ cups brown sugar
1½ cups old fashioned rolled oats
1 cup all-purpose flour

¾ cup fresh parmesan cheese, grated
1 teaspoon kosher salt
½ cup plus 2 Tablespoons unsalted butter

- ♥ Preheat oven to 375 degrees.
- ♥ Slice fruit into bite-sized pieces; Cut butter into small cubes.
- ♥ Lightly butter a 9 x 12-inch baking dish. Place fruit in the baking dish.
- ♥ In a bowl, combine sugar, oats, flour, cheese, and salt and mix.
- ♥ With a pastry cutter, quickly mix the bits of butter into the sugar mixture to form a coarse meal. The mixture should be loose and crumbly, so be sure to work quickly to avoid melting the butter.
- ♥ Gently sprinkle the topping mixture over the fruit.
- ♥ Bake for 35 minutes, or until the top is browned and the fruit is bubbly. Serve warm with a sprig of mint and vanilla bean ice cream. *Yum!*

Fourth of July Ice Cream

It really isn't summer until the ice cream has been made! Nana always made preparing this treat such a fun adventure for her grandsons, and they adored being in the kitchen making it with her. I add vanilla bean to make this summer treat even more flavorful.

Yield: One gallon

6 large eggs
2 cups granulated sugar
½ teaspoon salt
½ cup Karo corn syrup

1 pint half and half cream
1 Tablespoon pure vanilla extract
Vanilla beans from 2 bean pods
2 to 3 cups two-percent milk

- ♥ Whip eggs, sugar and salt for 10 minutes, or until light yellow in color.
- ♥ Mix in Karo, half and half, vanilla and vanilla bean.
- ♥ Pour into ice cream freezer and fill to ½ full.
- ♥ Fill remaining ½ with milk.
- ♥ Freeze per instructions with freezer.

OPTIONAL: For chocolate chip ice cream, add 2 to 4 ounces good quality semi-sweet chocolate, shaved, and do not include vanilla bean. -or-
Add fresh strawberries, peaches or berries for fruit flavored ice cream.

USING VANILLA BEAN

Choose shiny, black bean pods that are supple.
When purchasing vanilla beans, it is often hard to see the pods as they are packaged with labels that cover much of the ingredients. So shake the glass or jar containers to see it the bean pods rattle. If so, they have likely dried out and are not good. After opening container, store bean pods by wrapping tightly in plastic wrap inside a glass jar. Capture vanilla beans from the pod by slitting lengthwise and scraping out the copious tiny seeds with a knife.

Mama's Ice Cream Sandwiches

*Nothing says, "I love you" like an ice cream sandwich! Every kid on our block loves these irresistible summer sandwiches made from chewy chocolate cookies and Oklahoma Blue Bell ice cream. These are a "**Mrs. Waldeck**" specialty on South Cincinnati Avenue. When Robby was at Colorado College running for the Cross Country team, I took these treats on dry ice to the Oklahoma meet each year. They always took First Place!*

Yield: Twenty cookies; ten sandwiches (It's best to make a double batch!)

1¼ cups unsalted butter, softened
2 cups granulated sugar
2 large eggs
2 teaspoons pure vanilla extract
2 cups all-purpose flour

¾ cup good quality cocoa
1 teaspoon baking soda
½ teaspoon salt
1 gallon ice cream per batch

- ♥ Preheat oven to 350 degrees.
- ♥ Beat butter at medium speed with an electric mixer until creamy; gradually add sugar, beating well. Add eggs and vanilla, beating until well blended.
- ♥ Sift flour with cocoa, soda and salt; gradually add to butter mixture, beating at low speed until blended after each addition.
- ♥ Scoop dough into Tablespoon-sized balls and drop onto lightly greased cookie sheets. Use care to not over-crowd your cookie sheet, as these cookies spread and flatten quite a bit during baking.
- ♥ Bake for 18 minutes, or until lightly browned.
- ♥ Cool in pan just 1 to 2 minutes, then remove to wire racks covered with waxed paper to cool completely.
- ♥ Once cookies are cool, place a large scoop of (made in Oklahoma) Blue Bell vanilla bean and/or Blue Bell coffee ice cream onto cookie. Gently press a second cookie on top, then wrap in waxed paper and return to freezer for a few hours to set.

Cakes

CAKES

Christmas Morning Coffee Cake

Chocolate Sunflower with Pastry Cream

Dad's Decadent Chocolate Cake

Grandma's Strawberry Shortcake

Hoosier Sheet Cake

Luscious Lemon Layer Cake

Naples Nutella Pound Cake

Robby's Chocolate Birthday Cake

Todd's Italian Cream Cake

Buddy's DOGGIE Birthday Cake

Secrets for Light & Airy Cakes

Christmas Morning Coffee Cake

I like to bake this cake on Christmas morning and serve while un-wrapping gifts. The batter is dense, but the sour cream makes it moist and delicious. The sugar and nut filling add a little sweet crunch to every bite. Perfect with hot coffee!

Yield: One Bundt cake

CAKE

½ cup unsalted butter, softened
1 cup granulated sugar
2 large eggs
2 cups all-purpose flour
1 teaspoon baking powder

1 teaspoon baking soda
¼ teaspoon salt
12 ounces sour cream
1½ teaspoons pure vanilla extract

TOPPING

½ cup granulated sugar
1½ teaspoon cinnamon

½ cup hazelnuts

- ♥ Preheat oven to 350 degrees.
- ♥ Lightly toast and chop hazelnuts. In a small bowl, combine topping ingredients and set aside.
- ♥ In a large bowl with an electric mixer, cream butter and sugar thoroughly. Beat eggs well and add. Sift flour, baking powder, baking soda and salt in medium bowl. Mix sour cream and vanilla in small bowl.
- ♥ Add dry ingredients to egg mixture alternately with sour cream, working quickly to avoid over-mixing. Turn half of the batter into a greased and floured Bundt pan. Sprinkle on half of the topping mixture. Add remaining batter to pan with remaining topping on top.
- ♥ Bake 35 to 45 minutes, or until a toothpick inserted in center comes out clean. Allow cake to cool in Bundt pan for at least 30 minutes.

Chocolate Sunflower with Pastry Cream

As a young cook, I had the unforgettable opportunity to learn from a French born chef who was working in New York. She was amazing, and taught me some really neat tips for a more sophisticated kind of baking. From her I also learned the importance of always choosing the best ingredients, including good quality chocolate. I make this chocolate fudge cake in Lydie's honor. It is a dense cake accompanied by a light custard. The cake is served in the middle of a platter, with the custard poured around the outside, making it look just like a pretty sunflower.

Yield: One cake, serves eight

CAKE

1 Tablespoon Godiva chocolate liqueur
4½ ounces (good quality) bittersweet chocolate
4½ ounces unsalted butter
2 large eggs
½ cup hazelnuts, chopped

2/3 cup superfine sugar
1 Tablespoon all-purpose flour
1 Tablespoon butter to grease cake pan
Pastry Cream (See recipe on following page)

- ♥ Prepare a batch of Pastry Cream. Add 1 Tablespoon of Godiva chocolate liqueur. Chop nuts. Make superfine sugar if necessary (See instructions with *Candied Flowers* on page 177).
- ♥ Melt the chocolate in an uncovered double boiler. Be sure that no moisture gets into the chocolate, or it will "tighten" and be grainy. Should this happen, smooth it out with 2 teaspoons of Crisco shortening. Allow chocolate to cool to just above skin temperature. Test the temperature by dipping your finger into the chocolate and touching it to your lip. If it feels hot, the chocolate is too warm to mix with the butter.
- ♥ Place butter on parchment paper and knead with the palm of your hand until smooth.

- ♥ In a heavy mixer at medium speed, beat eggs and sugar until thick and foamy, about 8 minutes.
- ♥ When the chocolate has cooled, whisk it into the butter. The butter-chocolate must be thick, not runny. If it is runny, refrigerate until cold, then beat to aerate it.
- ♥ Beat the chocolate and butter mixture into the eggs and sugar, Tablespoon by Tablespoon. Fold in ½ cup of chopped hazelnuts, then sift 1 Tablespoon flour on top of the batter and fold in by hand with a rubber spatula.
- ♥ Preheat oven to 350 degrees.
- ♥ Butter an 8-inch round cake pan and line the bottom with buttered parchment paper that has been cut to fit the bottom of the pan. Pour the batter into the pan, then cover with buttered paper that has been cut to fit the top of the cake. This will keep it from drying out.
  To cut parchment paper exactly to pan size, use a pencil to trace the pan (top and bottom) then cut out the circle, taking care to ensure size is exact.
- ♥ Place the cake pan in a hot water bath about half as deep as the cake pan. Bake one hour.
- ♥ Remove pan from water bath. Remove the parchment paper from top of cake. Slide a knife around the edge of the pan to loosen the cake. Invert onto a serving platter with a large enough rim to accommodate the Pastry Cream and allow it to cool. Do not try to remove the cake from pan at this point; wait until the cake has cooled.
- ♥ When cool, unmold the cake (it will be quite flat). Remove the second sheet of paper. Pour the Pastry Cream around the cake and serve.

NOTE: The cake can be prepared in the morning and refrigerated. Bring back to room temperature before serving (allow about 2 hours).

Pastry Cream

This cream is good served over any chocolate cake or rum cake, as well as over fruit. Before making, assemble and measure all the ingredients so they are readily at hand.

Yield: Eight servings

2 Tablespoons cornstarch
2 Tablespoons all-purpose flour
½ cup granulated sugar
3 large egg yolks

3 cups milk
3 Tablespoons butter
2 Tablespoons Godiva liqueur

- ♥ Sift the cornstarch and flour into a large mixing bowl. Mix in the sugar; Set aside. Beat egg yolks lightly in separate bowl; Set aside.
- ♥ In a heavy-bottomed saucepan. Bring 3 cups of milk to a *rolling* boil over medium heat. Quickly pour half the boiling milk over the sugar, flour and cornstarch. Whisk vigorously. Whisk in the beaten egg yolks.
- ♥ Bring the other half of the milk back to a rolling boil, then pour into the custard mixture. Whisk over medium heat until the custard thickens. It binds within 10 seconds! Do not scrape the bottom and sides of the pan.
- ♥ Remove from heat, but continue whisking to cool the custard. Transfer to a mixing bowl to cool for 15 minutes.
- ♥ Meanwhile, cream 3 Tablespoons butter with the heel of your hand. Start whisking 1 Tablespoon of butter at a time into the custard. Whisk in 2 Tablespoons liqueur.
- ♥ Cover with plastic wrap. Refrigerate until ready to serve. Whisk again before serving.

EGGS

If your recipe calls for eggs to be at room temperature, you can speed up the process by placing them in a bowl of warm water for a few minutes.

When breaking eggs, be sure to capture all of the egg white that can sometimes cling to the shell. Simply use your index finger to gently scrap out any egg white still clinging to the inside.

Always remember to break eggs into a small bowl before adding to your batter and recipes so that you can check that eggs are not spoiled in any way and ensure no bits of shell slip in by accident.

Dad's Decadent Chocolate Cake

If you want a really special cake that is sure to both impress and delight, this is just the ticket. This tall, extra rich, three-layer cake is filled with a light, sweet almond cream and iced with semi-sweet chocolate. I liked to make this cake for my Dad on his birthday. Dad lived to 92 years, and had both a sweet tooth and taste for elegant cooking to the very end.

Yield: One cake, serves twenty

CAKE

1 cup unsweetened cocoa
2 cups boiling water
2¾ cups all-purpose flour
2 teaspoons baking soda
½ teaspoon salt

½ teaspoon baking powder
1 cup unsalted butter, softened
2½ cups granulated sugar
4 large eggs
1½ teaspoon pure vanilla extract

♥ Preheat oven to 350 degrees.
♥ Combine cocoa and boiling water and beat until smooth. Cool completely. Sift together three times the flour, salt, soda and baking powder. Set aside.
♥ In a large bowl with an electric mixer, cream butter, sugar, eggs and vanilla until light and fluffy, about 5 minutes. Add flour mixture alternately with cocoa mixture, beginning and ending with flour mixture. Do not overbeat or your batter will be tough.
♥ Grease and lightly flour three 9-inch cake pans. Divide cake batter evenly between pans. Bake for 25 to 30 minutes, or until toothpick inserted into center of cakes comes out clean. Cool in pans for 5 to 10 minutes, then remove. Carefully loosen sides of each cake with a knife and remove cakes to a cooling rack. Cool completely.

NOTE: Cakes tend to stick to pans if left in too long after removing from the oven. Unless otherwise instructed, cool cakes for only the first 5 to 10 minutes in the pans, and then remove to a wire rack to cool completely.

FILLING

1 cup heavy cream, chilled
¼ cup powdered sugar

1 teaspoon almond extract

♥ Whip cream until soft peaks form. Beat in sugar and almond. Refrigerate.

HOW TO WHIP CREAM

*Opposite of egg whites that should be beaten at room temperature,
cream should be chilled before whipping for best results.*

FROSTING

1 6-ounce package semi-sweet
chocolate chips
½ cup half and half cream

1 cup unsalted butter
2½ cups powdered sugar, sifted

♥ Sift powdered sugar to avoid lumps in icing. Combine chocolate chips, cream
and butter in a saucepan. Stir over medium heat until melted and smooth.
Remove from heat and whisk in powdered sugar. Place pan over ice and beat
with an electric mixer until frosting thickens and holds its shape, at least 5
minutes.

ASSEMBLY

♥ Place one layer topside down on a cake plate.
(The bottom of the cake will absorb the cream better and by placing the
stickier top of cake down first you prevent this very tall cake from
slipping off the plate.)
♥ Spread half the cream filling over cake. Repeat with the second layer.
♥ Place the third layer on top with the topside up. See *How to Frost a Cake* on
page 125, and frost as directed.
♥ Refrigerate at least 1 hour before serving. Keep any leftover cake
refrigerated.

OPTIONAL: The icing for this cake turns to a light chocolate brown when
whipped. The top is especially pretty when sprinkled with purple sugar
crystals and silver French dragées.

Grandma's Strawberry Shortcake

This rustic cake is a staple for Sunday night dinners when strawberries are in season. Crunchy on the outside and biscuit soft inside, the juice from the berries quickly absorbs into the cake making it deliciously sweet. This is my southern grandmother's recipe and one of the first cakes I learned to make. It always tastes like home.

Yield: Serves six to eight

2 cups all-purpose flour
1 teaspoon salt
4 teaspoons baking powder
1/3 cup unsalted butter, softened
5 Tablespoons granulated sugar

2/3 cup buttermilk
Butter for topping
2 pints ripe strawberries, sliced & sweetened with sugar
Milk

- ♥ Preheat oven to 425 degrees. Grease a 9 x 13 x ½-inch jelly roll pan.
- ♥ Sift to combine flour, **2 Tablespoons sugar**, baking powder and salt.
- ♥ With a pastry blender, cut butter into flour mixture until it resembles a coarse meal *(See photo at right)*.

- ♥ Using a fork, stir in the buttermilk until just blended.
- ♥ Place dough on jelly roll pan and spread evenly. Dough should be thick, but cover most of pan's surface.
- ♥ Sprinkle remaining sugar on top of cake and dot with butter *(See photo at right)*.

- ♥ Bake for 13 to 15 minutes, or until lightly golden.
- ♥ While the cake bakes, wash and

hull the berries. Then slice and sweeten with sugar to get the juices running.
Cover and refrigerate until ready to use.

TO SERVE:
- ♥ Break an approximate 3 x 3-inch square of cake into individual serving bowls and crumble lightly.
- ♥ Spoon strawberries and juice on top of each serving.
- ♥ Have a pitcher of cool milk on the table and encourage guests to add approximately ½ cup of milk to their shortcake before digging in.

For a more formal presentation, bake shortcake in two 8-inch cake pans. Assemble by placing sweetened berries between the two cake layers and on top, and then add a sprig of fresh mint to the center. Grandma would approve!

MAKING BUTTERMILK FROM SWEET MILK

If you do not have buttermilk on hand, you can make it.

Add 1 Tablespoon of white vinegar or lemon juice to 1 cup sweet milk.
Allow this mixture to stand at room temperature for 10 to 15 minutes
then add to recipe.

Hoosier Sheet Cake

This cake is a staple for every Indiana hostess. It is ultra-moist, super-chocolaty and can feed a crowd. The icing is applied while the cake is still warm, so it is absorbed in the top layer of the cake, making three layers of texture – super moist cake, sticky sweet top, and crisp and chocolaty thin icing. Nothin' better!

Yield: One sheet cake, approximately thirty-two bars

CAKE

1 cup water
¼ cup good quality cocoa
1 cup unsalted butter
2 cups all-purpose flour
½ cup buttermilk
2 large eggs

2 cups granulated sugar
1 teaspoon baking soda
½ teaspoon salt
1½ teaspoons pure vanilla extract
Cocoa Frosting (See recipe below)

- ♥ Preheat oven to 350 degrees. Grease and flour a 9 x 13 x ½-inch jelly roll pan.
- ♥ Heat water, cocoa and butter in small saucepan until the butter melts; set aside. Sift together flour, sugar, baking soda and salt.
- ♥ Add cocoa mixture to the dry ingredients then add the buttermilk, vanilla and eggs, one at a time.
- ♥ Bake for 20 to 25 minutes. Do not over bake.
- ♥ While cake is baking, make the frosting. Pour frosting over the cake and spread to even across the top while cake is still warm.

COCOA FROSTING

1/3 cup buttermilk
½ cup butter
¼ cup cocoa

1 pound powdered sugar, sifted
1 teaspoon pure vanilla extract

- ♥ Heat first three ingredients until bubbling; remove from heat.
- ♥ Add sugar and vanilla; blend until creamy.
- ♥ Pour/spread on warm cake. Cut into 32 bars.

Luscious Lemon Layer Cake

This light and lemony cake, layered with tangy lemon curd and coated with lemony butter frosting is an exceptional treat for any occasion. Be sure to use fresh lemons and make your own curd, as nothing compares to the fresh bright taste. You will need 4 to 5 fresh lemons for this recipe.

From Sweet Cakes, 2010

Yield: One cake, serves eight to ten

CAKE

2 1/3 cups cake flour, plus more to prepare pans
2¾ teaspoons baking powder
¼ teaspoon salt
1¾ cups granulated sugar
2 Tablespoons rind of lemon, grated

12 Tablespoons unsalted butter, softened, plus more to grease pans
1 cup whole milk
5 large egg whites
¼ teaspoon cream of tartar

- ♥ Set butter (for cake and frosting), milk and eggs on counter and bring to room temperature before beginning. Grate lemon rind.
- ♥ Preheat oven to 350 degrees and position rack in middle of oven. Generously butter and flour two 8-inch cake rounds.
- ♥ Sift cake flour with baking powder and salt three times; set aside. Pulse ¼ cup of the sugar with lemon zest in a food processor until well-combined.
- ♥ In a large bowl with an electric mixer, beat butter and lemon sugar until light and fluffy, approximately 1 to 2 minutes. Add remaining 1½ cups sugar and beat until smooth, another 1 to 2 minutes.
- ♥ Beat in ¼ of the milk until just blended.
- ♥ On low speed, add the flour mixture alternately with the remaining milk in three batches, scraping the bowl with each addition. Beat just until blended.
- ♥ In a separate large bowl, beat egg whites with an electric mixer (and clean, dry beaters) on medium speed just until foamy. Add the cream of tartar, increase speed to medium high, and beat until stiff peaks form when the beaters are lifted out.

- ♥ Add ¼ of the whites to the batter and gently fold them in with a spatula; continue to gently fold in whites, a quarter at a time, being careful to not deflate the mixture.
- ♥ Divide the batter evenly between the prepared pans. Gently swish cake pans to and fro on countertop to deflate any large air bubbles and to smooth top of cakes. Bake for 35 to 40 minutes, or until toothpick inserted into center comes out clean.
- ♥ Let cakes cool in pans for 5 to 10 minutes. Then run a knife around the inside of the pans and carefully invert onto a cooling rack flipped right side up. Cool completely.

LEMON CURD

½ cup unsalted butter
¾ cup granulated sugar
½ cup juice of fresh lemon

3 Tablespoons rind of lemon, grated
1/8 teaspoon salt
6 large egg yolks

- ♥ Melt butter in medium-sized saucepan over medium heat. Remove pan from heat and whisk in sugar, lemon juice, rind and salt. Whisk in the yolks until smooth.
- ♥ Return pan to medium heat and cook curd, whisking constantly, until the mixture thickens, 5 to 6 minutes. To check if curd is thick enough, dip a wooden spoon into it and draw your finger across the back of the spoon; your finger should leave a path. Be sure to not allow the mixture to boil. Refrigerate covered, until ready to use.

FROSTING

1 cup unsalted butter, softened
2 Tablespoons rind of lemon, grated

3½ cups powdered sugar, sifted
3 Tablespoons juice of fresh lemon

- ♥ In a medium bowl, beat the butter and lemon rind with an electric mixer on medium speed until light and fluffy.
- ♥ Add the powdered sugar in batches and beat until light and fluffy.
- ♥ Add the lemon juice and beat for 1 minute.

NOTE: Frosting can be made a couple hours ahead, and kept covered and cool (but not cold), until ready to use. Be sure to allow a few hours before serving cake to assemble and chill as directed.

GRATING LEMON RIND

To grate lemon or orange rind, gently run whole fruit up and down a micro plane or grater. For strips of rind, use a vegetable peeler.

Rather than composting lemon and orange rinds, grind them in garbage disposal and your kitchen will smell citrus fresh!

ASSEMBLY

- With the palm of one hand gently pressed on top of cake layer, cut each in half horizontally, using a long serrated knife.
- Put one of the four cake layers on a pretty cake plate, cut side up.
- With a spatula, spread a generous 1/3 cup of the chilled curd on top of cake layer. Lay another layer on top, spread it with another generous 1/3 cup of curd, and repeat with the third layer and last 1/3 cup of curd. Top with the fourth cake layer, top side up.

TO FROST

- Spread a thin layer of frosting on the cake, filling in any gaps as you go. Chill cake until the frosting firms, about ½ hour.
- Spread the remaining frosting decoratively over the top and sides of the cake with a long offset spatula, designed for icing cakes.
- Use a damp paper towel to clean excess frosting and cake crumbs from cake plate.

TWO WAYS TO FROST

1) *Leave icing white and scatter top with bits of grated lemon and French dragées or Candied Violets (See page 177). -or-*
2) *Divide frosting into three parts. Color the frosting purple, aqua and pink (as is shown on chapter cover page) or any combination of three colors that please you. Then sprinkle top of cake with crystals and sprinkles.*
   You can find neat sprinkles and crystals in any specialty baking shop.

Naples Nutella-Swirl Pound Cake

We first discovered Nutella, a delicious chocolate hazelnut spread, while on our way to the Isle of Capri in Italy. This dense pound cake has a Nutella center and is scrumptious served warm!

Yield: One Bundt cake

1½ cups all-purpose flour, plus more for dusting
4 large eggs, at room temperature
2 teaspoons pure vanilla extract
¾ teaspoon baking powder
¼ teaspoon salt

1 cup unsalted butter, softened
1¼ cups granulated sugar
1 13-ounce jar chocolate-hazelnut spread
½ cup hazelnuts, chopped fine

- ♥ Preheat oven to 325 degrees.
- ♥ Lightly grease and flour Bundt pan, tapping out any excess flour. Mix chopped hazelnuts with spread and set aside.
- ♥ In a small bowl, lightly beat the eggs with the vanilla. In a medium bowl, sift flour with the baking powder and salt.
- ♥ In a large bowl, using an electric mixer, beat the butter with the sugar at medium high speed until fluffy, about 3 minutes. With the mixer at medium-low speed, gradually beat in the egg mixture until fully and well incorporated. Add the flour mixture in 3 batches, beating at low speed between additions until just incorporated. Continue to beat for 30 seconds longer, being careful not to overbeat.
- ♥ Spread one-third of the batter in the prepared pan, then spread half of the Nutella and nut mixture on top. Repeat with another third of the batter and the remaining Nutella mixture. Top with the remaining batter. Lightly swirl the Nutella into the batter by inserting and dragging a butter knife. Do not over mix. Bake the cake for about 1 hour and 15 minutes, or until a toothpick inserted in the center comes out clean. Let the cake cool in the pan for 25 to 30 minutes.
- ♥ Invert the cake onto a wire rack, turn it right side up and let cool completely (approximately 2 hours). Or, serve warm after 30 minutes.

Robby's Chocolate Birthday Cake

*I found this recipe in a magazine when my boys were little. It was described as the perfect after school treat, so I made it that afternoon and had it waiting for Robby and Michael when they came home from school. The moist, chocolaty butter cake is perfect with a glass of milk, and won big points with my boys. In fact, **Robby** liked it so much it became his birthday cake, served each year.*

Yield: One three-layer cake

CAKE

1 cup unsalted butter, softened
1¾ cups granulated sugar
1 Tablespoon pure vanilla extract
3 large eggs
1 cup good quality, unsweetened cocoa
2¼ cups all-purpose flour

1 teaspoon baking soda
1½ teaspoon baking powder
¼ teaspoon salt
1¾ cups milk
Fudge Frosting (See recipe on following page)

♥ Preheat oven to 350 degrees. Grease and flour three 8-inch cake rounds.
♥ In a large bowl, with an electric mixer, cream together butter, sugar and vanilla until light and fluffy. Add eggs *one at a time*; mixing until well combined.
♥ Measure flour, then sift together (three times) with cocoa, baking soda, baking powder and salt onto a piece of waxed paper.
♥ Add to butter mixture alternately with milk, mixing just until well combined. Divide batter evenly into three prepared pans.
♥ Bake for 25 to 30 minutes, or until a toothpick inserted into center comes out clean. Cool 5 to 10 minutes in pans; remove from pans to cooling rack and cool completely. Fill and frost.

CAKE FLOUR

Cake flour makes a lighter, more crumbly cake.

If your recipe calls for cake flour and you do not have it on hand,
use 2 Tablespoons *less* all-purpose flour for each cup of cake flour specified.

FUDGE FROSTING

1 cup unsalted butter, softened
4 cups powdered sugar, sifted
½ cup unsweetened cocoa

2 teaspoons pure vanilla extract
4 to 5 Tablespoons milk

♥ Beat all ingredients in large bowl with electric mixer until smooth and fluffy.
♥ Frost between each layer, top and sides of cake.

OPTIONAL: Top cakes with curls of shaved chocolate mounded in the center.
This is especially pretty with a mix of dark, milk and white chocolate.

MAKING CHOCOLATE CURLS

Chocolate curls are pretty mounded atop cakes.

Corkscrew curls: Draw a vegetable peeler across the sides of a chocolate bar,
applying steady pressure. If your chocolate is brittle and breaks before it curls,
warm it in your apron pocket for a few minutes. Too soft to curl? Pop chocolate
bar in the refrigerator.

Broad curls: Melt 2 ounces of chocolate (2 ounces will make 8 to 10 curls). When
just melted, spread a thin layer onto the bottom of a glass baking dish. When
firm but not hard, place the blade of a metal spatula at a 45 degree angle onto
chocolate and apply gentle, steady pressure as you push the spatula forward in
half-circles. Control the tightness or looseness of curls with the angle of your
spatula. A 30 degree angle will create a looser cone-shaped fan of curls. Use
excess shards as accents to curls. Transfer curls with your spatula, not warm
hands, to a plate and refrigerate until ready to use.

Todd's Italian Cream Cake

There are many versions of Italian Cream Cake, but this is my favorite because it is iced like a torte. The cream cheese frosting is placed only between the coconut cake layers, thus preventing the cake from being overly sweet.

My husband *often requests this cake for his birthday. It is a little involved, and takes two hours from start to finish, but is worth the time and always gets a rave review. Happy Birthday Todd!*

Yield: One three-layer cake

CAKE

2 cups granulated sugar
½ cup unsalted butter, softened
½ cup Crisco shortening
5 large eggs, separated

2 cups all-purpose flour
1 cup buttermilk
1 teaspoon baking soda
1 3½-ounce can Angel Flake coconut

- ♥ Preheat oven to 350 degrees. Separate eggs into two bowls.
- ♥ Beat egg whites (at room temperature) until stiff; set aside. Cream sugar, butter and shortening until light and fluffy.
- ♥ Add egg **yolks,** one at a time. Add soda to buttermilk and add alternately with sifted flour. Add coconut. Beat well.
- ♥ By hand, fold in 5 beaten egg **whites,** being careful to not over-mix and deflate whites. Divide batter evenly into three greased and floured 8-inch cake pans. Bake for 25 minutes. Cool and frost.

FROSTING

1 8-ounce package cream cheese
½ cup unsalted butter, softened
1½ teaspoon pure vanilla extract

1 cup toasted & chopped nuts
(pecans or hazelnuts)
1 1-pound box powdered sugar

- ♥ Mix cream cheese, butter and vanilla; sift sugar and add, blending well. Add nuts; blend well. Frost only the top layer of each cake, leaving sides bare like a torte.

124

HOW TO FROST A CAKE

Creating picture-perfect cakes can be accomplished in five easy steps.

Position & level your cake

Set your cake plate on a Lazy Susan or use a cake plate with a pedestal so it can be rotated easily and avoid possible jarring. Place the first cake layer upside down. Because the top of a cake is sticky, this will prevent the layers from slipping off of each other, and your plate!

Fill the layers

Dust your cake for any excess crumbs using a long, offset spatula knife designed for icing cakes (this purchase is worth the investment if you like to bake). Spread the filling evenly on top of the first layer; don't worry about getting the frosting smooth. Place the second layer on the frosting and align the layers. Add additional layers if you have them, ending with the top layer unfrosted.

Seal in the crumbs

Spread a very thin layer of frosting over the sides of your cake to seal in the crumbs. Place cake in the refrigerator at this point to set-up (about 20 to 30 minutes). Once your thin layer is set, finish frosting the cake with remaining icing.

Finish with flair

Spread the remaining frosting evenly over the sides and top of cake. Use your knife lengthwise to spread the icing on the sides of your cake to create even and smooth sides. Then swirl the top of your masterpiece to create an interesting design with the frosting, dipping your knife up to create peaks and texture in the swirls.

Clean your plate

Finally, take a slightly damp paper towel and wipe any remaining crumbs, smudges and excess frosting from the plate. Top cake with candied flowers, shaved lemon rind or chocolate curls as desired.

Buddy's DOGGIE Birthday Cake

*This cookbook could not be complete without sharing my birthday cake for **Buddy** – our Cavalier King Charles Spaniel. This doggie cake is sure to please, and includes ingredients like peanut butter and carrots that dogs love. Yappy Bark Day!*

Yield: Serves one cute puppy and his/her canine friends

CAKE

1 large egg
¼ cup peanut butter (not crunchy)
¼ cup cooking oil
1/3 cup honey

1 cup carrots, shredded
1 cup whole wheat flour
1 teaspoon baking soda

- ♥ Preheat oven to 350 degrees. Grease a small Bundt pan or miniature cake pan.
- ♥ Combine egg, peanut butter, oil and honey in a large bowl.
- ♥ Stir in the carrots and mix thoroughly. Combine flour with soda and fold into carrot mixture. Spoon cake into prepared pan and bake for 35 to 40 minutes, or until toothpick inserted into middle comes out clean.
- ♥ Let cake cool in pan for 10 minutes; then turn out onto a plate and cool. Ice and serve!

ICING

1 cup honey

1/8 cup very warm water

- ♥ Dissolve honey in warm water.
- ♥ Drizzle over top and sides of cake while it is still warm.

126

Secrets for Light & Airy Cake

In our youth, 4-H was a big part of the summer for my sister and me. In girls 4-H, we learned to separate eggs, sift flour and other baking secrets for light and airy cakes. Our mom and her sister (Aunt Dude) and our cousin Sandy were our mentors and teachers. During the Cass County fair each August, we not only showed our ponies in Boy's 4-H, but baked cakes, breads and other treats in a county-wide competition. These are secrets I learned from my 4-H experience… and many baking experiences since then.

BUTTER TEMPERATURE

Most baking recipes call for the butter to be softened, or at room temperature. This is because the purpose of creaming butter is to beat tiny air bubbles into it to result in a light and airy cake. Butter holds air bubbles best at approximately 68 degrees. For best results, let your butter sit on the counter 20 to 30 minutes before beginning your cake. You will know when your butter is ready when your finger can easily make an indent in the stick. *To speed the softening process, place butter in a sealed plastic bag and gently pound with a rolling pin, or place baggie in a bowl of warm water.*

ADDING EGGS SEPARTELY

Another way to ensure a light cake with a fluffy texture is to add eggs separately. When recipes call for adding eggs one at a time, it is because this helps keep the batter blended and creamy, which is important to the final texture. If you add the eggs all at once, the batter can break and look curdled because your air pockets have collapsed. When this happens, your cake will taste okay, but will not be light and airy.

CREAMING BUTTER & SUGAR

Creaming the butter and sugar is important for a light cake. With an electric mixer, you can cut the sugar into the butter and create tiny air bubbles. A common mistake is to cream too little. You should continue creaming the butter and sugar until the mixture grows in volume and lightens to a pale yellow color. This may take as long as five minutes. Scrape the sides of your bowl once during the creaming process, and watch the batter, stopping if the butter begins to look curdled.

OVERMIXING

Over mixing your cake batter will destroy the air bubbles you've incorporated and will result in a cake that is tough and heavy. To avoid this, start with the mixer on low speed and stop it when most of the flour has been incorporated. At this point, remove the bowl from the mixer and finish mixing by hand with a spatula. This way you can both scrape the bottom of the bowl to get any pockets of flour and avoid unnecessary strokes.

THE WET-DRY METHOD OF BAKING

When recipes call for mixing all the dry ingredients in one bowl and wet (liquid) ingredients in another, it is designed to prevent the formation of gluten, which can make cakes heavy. By adding the liquids to the dry ingredients in batches, you are allowing the fat in your recipe to coat all the flour proteins and are preventing the formation of gluten. The wet-dry method results in cakes that are very tender. Be sure to always follow the method specified in your recipe to guarantee the correct results.

THE SIFTING QUANDRY

Most flour sack labels claim the contents to be pre-sifted. However, you have no way of knowing how long ago it was milled. Flour compacts as it stands so to be safe, be sure to always freshen your flour by sifting, three times, after measuring. Likewise, always use a dry measuring cup and a knife to level your measurement as opposed to shaking your measuring cup to level the flour. If you are also adding a leavener like baking powder or soda to your recipe, sift it along with the flour to thoroughly blend all ingredients and ensure your flour is not compact. And just like flour, be cognizant of soda and powder to ensure you are always using fresh. *To ensure your baking ingredients stay as fresh as possible, store in the freezer until ready to use.*

TO BEAT OR NOT TO BEAT

Be sure to start with room temperature eggs and pay close attention when beating egg whites. As whites whip, their color changes from very pale yellow to white. Properly beaten whites will look smooth, wet, and shiny, and will form soft peaks when the beaters are raised out of the bowl. If in doubt, it is preferable to under beat egg whites, because whites that have been overbeaten will appear lumpy and form big white clumps when you fold then into your batter mixture. Because their air bubbles have been overworked, they are more likely to collapse in the oven which will make your cake chewy rather than tender. *A neat trick for cleaning beaters when finished beating egg whites and mixing cakes or icings, is to very slowly raise them from the batter while mixer is still running. The egg white, batter or icing will whisk itself off as the beaters are raised up and out.*

PREPARING CAKE PANS

Buttering the bottom of cake pans, or using cooking spray, does not always guarantee a clean release. Using parchment paper along with buttering your pan, will guarantee your cakes do not stick to the pan and break apart when you are trying to remove them. Coating your pan with butter will also help prevent the paper from sliding and curling up when the batter is added. Another tip is to only allow cakes to cool in the pan for the first five to ten minutes. Once the pans have cooled enough to handle, remove cakes to a cooling rack to cool completely. And be sure to only butter the bottom of your layer cake pans. Cakes will naturally release from the sides of pans during baking, and buttering them will cause your batter to slide down, preventing your cake from rising to its fullest.

FILLING CAKE PANS

Be sure to fill pans only two-thirds full. Spread the batter in a circular motion with a spatula, then gently swish pans to and fro on the countertop a few times to remove any large air bubbles and assuring a smooth texture for your cake.

TESTING TO SEE IF YOUR CAKE IS DONE

My preferred method for testing cakes is to insert a toothpick into the center of the cake. If the pick comes out clean, the cake is done. If you see nothing, or just a few crumbs, remove cake from the oven and place on a cooling rack. If still-wet batter clings to the pick, return to the oven and set your timer for just a few minutes more and check again. Always stay near the kitchen when baking cakes to monitor the last ten minutes of baking time, especially. When you begin to smell the cake, it is nearly done.

To remove cakes from pans, run a knife around the edge of the pan, loosening any pieces of cake that are clinging. Gently use your knife to partially lift and loosen cake from bottom of pans as well. Then place inverted cake plate or cooling rack on top of cake pan and quickly flip while holding together. Once the cake is right side up, gently lift the cake pan off.

Even though it adds a step, lining the bottoms of cake pans with parchment paper (buttering pans before and after paper placement) is the best way to prevent cakes from breaking apart when removing from pans. *To ensure your paper is exactly the same size as the bottom of your pan, trace the bottom of pan onto paper with a pencil then carefully cut out the rounds.*

USING A KITCHEN TIMER
Always set your kitchen timer to check cakes about ¾ of the way through established cooking time. Rotate your pans at this juncture to ensure even baking, and double check that the cakes are not overcooking. If one side of your cake is browning unevenly, it is because it is too close to the side of your oven, so rotate the pan and adjust accordingly. There is often as much as a ten minute time difference in recipes and given the way your oven cooks. It's always better to be safe than sorry, for nothing is more disappointing than a cake that has baked too long and become dry. *If your oven is convection (preferred when baking) the cooking temperature is lower than what is recommended for a conventional oven. Newer ovens calculate the difference automatically.*

Pies & Tarts

PIES & TARTS

Amish Cream Pie

Blackberry Pie

Christmas Cranberry Tart

Classic Apple Pie

Coconut Cream Tarts, Macadamia Nut Crusts

French Strawberry Glacé Pie

Holiday Pie with Braided Crust

Lemon Meringue Pie

Peach Pie

Waldeck Chocolate Pie

Gladdie's Pie Crust

Amish Cream Pie

This custard pie recipe is from an Amish community in northern Indiana. The sweet creamy filling is topped with a sprinkling of cinnamon, and as my brother-in-law Chris will attest, it is worth fighting for!

Yield: One pie

PIE CRUST

1/3 recipe Gladdie's Pie Dough made into empty shell and baked.

CREAM FILLING

¼ **cup cornstarch**
1 **cup granulated sugar**
2 **cups half and half cream**

½ **cup unsalted butter**
1 **teaspoon pure vanilla extract**

- ♥ Preheat oven to 350 degrees.
- ♥ Mix cornstarch with sugar in a medium sauce pan; add cream. Cook until thick, whisking constantly. Add butter and continue cooking until melted and incorporated. Remove from heat and add vanilla.
- ♥ Pour cream mixture into a 9-inch baked pie shell. Sprinkle with cinnamon. Bake for 15 minutes longer, or until cream begins to bubble.
- ♥ Serve pie at room temperature.

BAKING PIE SHELLS

Many pies with a pudding or gelatin filling call for baking the pie crust empty first. The trick to doing so is to add some weight.

Begin by pricking the pie crust all over with a fork; this helps prevent it from puffing up while it bakes. Then place a slightly smaller aluminum pie tin inside the shell for the first few minutes of baking to prevent the middle and sides from slipping down.

Bake the crust in a preheated 375°F oven for 12 to 15 minutes. After 8 to 10 minutes, you can remove the smaller tin and allow the crust brown.

Blackberry Pie

Bake this pie in the month of June, when Blackberries are in season. There is nothing better!

Yield: One pie

½ recipe Gladdie's Pie Dough

4 cups fresh, juicy blackberries
3/4 cup granulated sugar, plus more for topping

¼ cup all-purpose flour
1 teaspoon juice of fresh lemon
3 pats unsalted butter

- ♥ Preheat oven to 375 degrees.
- ♥ Coat berries with lemon juice. Combine sugar and flour and mix with berries to coat. (Adjust amount of sugar and berries according to sweetness and juiciness of berries.)
- ♥ Mound berries into a chilled and un-baked pie shell and dot with three pats of butter. Add top crust, crimp edges, vent, and sprinkle with sugar.
- ♥ Bake for 45 minutes to 1 hour, or until crust is browned and filling is bubbly.

The pictures above show the preparation steps for one small individual-sized pie:
Coating fruit with sugar and flour; dotting pie with butter; crimping edges to seal.

Christmas Cranberry Tart

I grew up in the small north central Indiana town of Logansport where making a good pie earned a badge of honor. This cranberry tart became "Katy's" first accolade as I joined in the ranks of good Adams family cooks. It is pretty, red, and perfect for Christmas Eve. The tart filling with the sweet, nutty crust is an unexpected combination.

Yield: Two nine-inch pies, twelve three-inch tarts or thirty-six individual tartlettes

NUT CRUST

5 ounces almonds, finely chopped
5 ounces pecans, finely chopped
1 cup unsalted butter
1/3 cup granulated sugar

3 cups all-purpose flour
1 large egg, beaten
1 teaspoon almond extract

- ♥ Preheat oven to 350 degrees.
- ♥ Mix all ingredients into a dough and press into the bottom and sides of a tart pan(s).
- ♥ Chill shell(s) for 20 minutes while making filling.
- ♥ Bake shell(s) for 15 to 20 minutes after chilling.

FILLING

1 envelope gelatin softened in
¼ cup cold water
3 cups fresh cranberries

1 cup granulated sugar
½ cup+ red currant jelly

- ♥ Combine sugar, cranberries and jelly in saucepan. Cook approximately 20 minutes, or until berries are tender, yet firm. Cool mixture for 20 minutes.
- ♥ Add gelatin to cooled berries and mix well. Pour into baked and cooled crust. Chill before serving.

Classic Apple Pie

*This is the pie **my mother Gladys** was best known for. Every time mom served apple pie to company, she was encouraged to open her own pie shop. Fresh-picked juicy apples make this pie delicious, and part of the fun of baking pie with mom was going to the apple orchard in search of the best fruits. She liked to make an adventure of the trip, taking the country roads and buying bushel baskets of apples, Indiana corn and tomatoes along the way. The Indiana orchard owners all knew mom by name because she was so friendly and got such a kick out of visiting with the folks on the farm. When I bake apple pie, I like to mix my favorite apples and chop them into cubes, rather than slicing, to ensure each bite is well coated with cinnamon and sugar.*

Yield: One pie

½ recipe Gladdie's Pie Dough

4 granny smith apples
4 jonathan apples
***1 to 1½ cups granulated sugar, plus more for topping pie**
***3 to 4 Tablespoons all-purpose flour**

1/8 teaspoon salt
¾ teaspoon cinnamon
½ teaspoon nutmeg
Juice of ½ fresh lemon
3 pats unsalted butter

- ♥ Preheat oven to 500 degrees.
- ♥ Peel, core and cube apples, leaving skin on the jonathans. Coat apples with fresh lemon juice. Mix sugar, flour, salt, cinnamon and nutmeg; coat apples.
- ♥ Mound apples into a chilled and un-baked pie shell and dot with 3 pats of butter. Add top crust, crimp edges, cut vents, and sprinkle with sugar.
- ♥ Bake 500 degrees for 8 minutes. Reduce heat to 350 degrees and bake for 1 hour, or until crust is browned and filling is bubbly.

NOTES:
1) *See *Baking Fruit Pies* in this chapter.
2) If jonathan apples are not available, use seven granny smiths.

USING PIE SHIELDS

Remember to place fruit pies on a pie shield sheet, to avoid juice over flow onto oven.

* If you do not have a pie shield (a thin, round cooking sheet with the center removed), place strips of foil on your oven rack to form a circle just larger than your pie plate. Leave the center of the circle open to encourage bottom crust to cook completely.

Remember to also use a pie crust shield when baking any pie. Shield pie crusts during the first half of baking to prevent your crust from cooking faster than the pie.

*If you do not have a pie crust shield, you can easily make a shield with aluminum foil. Simply tear off about a 12-inch piece of foil, fold the piece in half, and tear in two. Fold these two strips in half lengthwise.
With side of your hand, indent the strips to form half circles, and then carefully fit over crust, being careful to not crush the dough.
Crimp two pieces of foil together to hold in place.

Should your pies overflow onto your oven floor and the juices begin to burn, throw salt onto the spill to stop the smoke.

If you do not have a pie crust shield, you can easily make a shield with aluminum foil.

1) Indent the strips to form half circles and shape around crust.
2) Crimp pieces together to hold in place as shield.

Coconut Cream Tarts with Macadamia Nut Crusts

*This is an elegant substitute for traditional coconut cream pie. The nut crust offsets the creamy filling and the macadamia nuts are perfect with the coconut. I make this for **my sister Jane**, who loves coconut cream.*

Yield: One dozen tarts

FILLING

1/3 cup all-purpose flour
¾ cup granulated sugar
4 large eggs

2 cups milk
1 Tablespoon pure vanilla extract
1½ cups flaked coconut, divided.

- ♥ Preheat oven to 350 degrees.
- ♥ Stir together flour and sugar; whisk eggs.
- ♥ Cook milk in a heavy saucepan over medium heat until hot. Gradually whisk about ¼ of hot milk into egg mixture to temper; then add to remaining hot milk, whisking constantly. Cook over medium-high heat, whisking constantly, 5 to 6 minutes or until thickened.
- ♥ Remove from heat; stir in vanilla and 1 cup coconut. Cover and **chill 3 hours.**
- ♥ Bake remaining ½ cup coconut in shallow pan in oven, stirring and watching so it does not burn, 4 to 5 minutes; set aside.

MACDAMIA NUT CRUST

2½ cups all-purpose flour
¾ cup cold unsalted butter

2 Tablespoons water
1½ cups macadamia nuts

- ♥ Cut butter into small cubes. Finely chop nuts.

- Pulse flour and butter in a food processor until crumbly. Add water, and pulse 30 seconds or until dough forms a ball. Turn out onto a lightly floured surface; knead in nuts.
- Divide dough into 12 equal portions; press each portion into a 3 to 4-inch tart pan. Prick bottoms with fork, and place on a 15 x 10-inch jellyroll pan. Cover with plastic wrap and **freeze 30 minutes**.
- Preheat oven to 375 degrees.
- Bake tarts on jellyroll pan for 15 to 20 minutes, or until golden. Cool in tart pans for five minutes; remove from pans, and cool completely on a wire rack.
- Spoon coconut custard mixture into tart shells.

TOPPING

1 cup whipping cream   **3 Tablespoons sugar**

- Beat **cold** whipping cream and sugar at high speed with an electric mixer until soft peaks form; dollop onto cooled tarts; chill until ready to serve.
- Just before serving, sprinkle each tart with toasted coconut.

NOTE: Total preparation time is 4 hours. Three hours need be allowed for pudding to chill and ½ hour allowed for dough to set.

French Strawberry Glacé Pie

This fresh strawberry pie has a hidden surprise of cream cheese lining the bottom crust. With just the right amount of gelatin, it really shows off the berries.

Yield: One pie

1/3 recipe Gladdie's Pie Dough
3-ounce package cream cheese, softened

FILLING

1 quart fresh strawberries (4 cups)
2/3 cup water

1 cup granulated sugar
3 Tablespoons cornstarch

- ♥ Bake pie shell at 375 degrees for 12 to 15 minutes or until golden brown; cool. Spread softened cream cheese over bottom of shell.
- ♥ Wash and hull strawberries, reserving ½ cup of choice berries.
- ♥ Simmer 1 cup of strawberries with 2/3 cups water for approximately 3 minutes. Blend sugar with cornstarch and add to boiling mixture; cook for 1 minute, stirring constantly. Cool mixture.
- ♥ Place remaining 2½ cups strawberries in pie shell and cover with cooked sugar mixture. Garnish top of pie with reserved berries.
- ♥ Refrigerate until firm, approximately 2 hours.

OPTIONAL: Serve with sweetened whipped cream.

Holiday Pie

This is the pie I am always asked to make during the holidays. It combines the perfect pecan pie with the perfect pumpkin pie. The fresh lemon provides pizazz. Because I love pie crust, I use a braided crust on this pie. It is not only a unique and pretty look, but provides more yummy crust to enjoy with each slice.

Yield: One scrumptious pie

½+ recipe Gladdie's Pie Dough
This allows for a braided crust and decorative cuts-outs.

- ♥ Roll half of the pie dough to 1/8-inch thick and fit into 9-inch pie plate.
- ♥ Braid remaining crust and adhere to rim of pie in plate per instructions on following page. Chill shell while making filling.

PUMPKIN LAYER

¾ cup canned pure pumpkin puree
2 Tablespoons packed light brown sugar
1 large egg, beaten lightly

2 Tablespoons sour cream
1/8 teaspoon cinnamon
1/8 teaspoon ground nutmeg

- ♥ Preheat oven to 425 degrees.
- ♥ In a small bowl whisk together ingredients for pumpkin layer until mixture is smooth.

PECAN LAYER

¾ cup light corn syrup
½ cup packed light brown sugar
3 large eggs, beaten lightly
3 Tablespoons unsalted butter
2 teaspoons pure vanilla extract

¼ teaspoon rind of lemon, grated
1½ teaspoons juice of fresh lemon
¼ teaspoon salt
1½ cups pecans, chopped

- ♥ Melt butter and cool. Grate lemon rind. Chop nuts.
- ♥ In another small bowl, combine well all ingredients for pecan layer except pecans. Stir in pecans.

ASSEMBLY

- ♥ Spread pumpkin mixture evenly in chilled pie shell and spoon pecan mixture over it carefully.
- ♥ Cover crust with pie crust shield or aluminum foil. Bake pie in upper third of 425-degree oven for 20 minutes.
- ♥ Reduce heat to 350 degrees, remove foil, and bake for 20 to 30 minutes more, until the filling is puffed slightly and crust is browned. The center will not appear to be quite set. Cool on rack.

NOTE: Pie can also be baked one day ahead and chilled, loosely covered with plastic wrap in the refrigerator. Reheat in a preheated 350-degree oven until crust is crisp, about 15 minutes.

OPTIONAL GARNISH: Top unbaked pie with holly-shaped cut outs of dough at Christmas time and maple leaves at Thanksgiving.

BRAIDING PIE CRUST

A braided crust takes roughly the same amount of dough as needed for a single crust pie.

Roll dough to 1/8-inch and cut into three 8-inch strips.
Braid three strips at a time by flipping and lapping the sides over the middle strip. Place strips on rim of pie crust after scoring both the bottom of braid and rim. Gently press strips to rim of pie crust to ensure they are adhered to pie, as well as individual braids to each other, for a seamless braid all around. Use 1-inch strips of dough crosswise to cover areas where two braids have been joined.

One pie typically needs four strips of braid.

Lemon Meringue Pie

The tart filling and sugary meringue makes a perfect pie, especially when coupled with my mother's pie crust.

Yield: One pie

1/3 recipe Gladdie's Pie Dough

- ♥ Bake 9-inch pie shell at 375 degrees for 12 to 15 minutes, or until browned. Let cool before filling.

LEMON FILLING

1½ cups granulated sugar
1½ cups water
½ teaspoon salt
½ cup cornstarch
1/3 cup water

4 large egg yolks, slightly beaten
½ cup juice of fresh lemon
3 Tablespoons unsalted butter
1 teaspoon rind of lemon, grated

- ♥ Combine sugar, 1½ cups water and salt in saucepan. Heat to boiling.
- ♥ Mix cornstarch and 1/3 cup water to make a smooth paste. Add to boiling mixture gradually, stirring constantly. Cook until thick and clear. Remove from heat and set aside.
- ♥ Combine egg yolks and lemon juice. Stir into thickened mixture. Return to heat and cook, stirring constantly until mixture bubbles again. Remove from heat. Stir in butter and lemon rind.
- ♥ Cover and cool until lukewarm.

NOTE: ½ cup of fresh lemon juice requires 1½ lemons.

MERINGUE

4 large egg whites
¼ teaspoon salt

½ cup granulated sugar

- ♥ Preheat oven to 325 degrees.

- Bring eggs whites to room temperature. Add salt to egg whites. Beat until frothy. Gradually add ½ cup sugar, beating until stiff, glossy peaks are formed.
- Stir 2 rounded Tablespoons of meringue into lukewarm filling. Pour filling into cool pie shell. Pile remaining meringue on top and spread lightly over filling, spreading to seal the edges to crust and mounding in the center. Sprinkle meringue lightly with sugar.
- Bake for about 15 minutes, or until lightly browned. Cool on rack at least one hour before cutting.

SECRET TO A GOOD MERINGUE

Use room temperature eggs for meringue, and add the sugar very slowly, so as not to defeat the meringue.
Also, be sure to always use clean and dry beaters.

Peach Pie

This is the pie my mother always made especially for me. Mom kept fresh peaches year-round by freezing batches each summer. Seasonal, juicy and sweet peaches are a must.

Yield: One pie
½ **recipe Gladdie's Pie Dough**

8 to 12 juicy and sweet peaches
¾ to 1 cup granulated sugar, plus more for topping pie
4 Tablespoons all-purpose flour

Juice of ½ fresh lemon
1/8 teaspoon cinnamon – just a hint
3 pats unsalted butter

- Preheat oven to 375 degrees.
- Combine dry ingredients. Coat peaches with fresh lemon juice. Combine coated peaches with sugar and flour mixture. Mound peaches into a chilled and un-baked pie shell, dot with butter. Add top crust, crimp edges, vent, and sprinkle with sugar.
- Bake until crust is browned and filling is bubbly: 45 minutes to 1 hour.

Waldeck Chocolate Pie

This pie was originally made by my husband's Grandmother Jane, and is a family favorite. Early in our engagement when visiting Todd's parents, my future mother-in-law would often urge me into the kitchen before the rest of the house was awake to teach me how to make my fiancé's favorite foods and desserts. Learning to make this pie is an especially memorable early morning lesson.

1/3 recipe Gladdie's Pie Dough

- ♥ Bake 9-inch pie shell at 375 degrees for 12 to 15 minutes, or until golden brown.

CHOCOLATE PUDDING

1 12-ounce can Milnot	3 large egg yolks
1½ cups milk	4 Tablespoons unsalted butter

- ♥ Cook Milnot and milk slowly. Add eggs and butter and continue slowly cooking, whisking constantly, just to boiling stage.
- ♥ In a separate bowl combine the following:

6 Tablespoons cocoa	1/8 teaspoon salt
1½ cups granulated sugar	Water (just enough to mix)
4½ Tablespoons cornstarch	1 teaspoon pure vanilla extract

- ♥ Stir together dry ingredients with just enough water to mix.
- ♥ Add chocolate mixture to milk mixture and continue to cook and whisk until boiling and thick. Remove from heat and stir in vanilla.
- ♥ Cool completely before assembling pie.

145

Gladdie's Pie Crust

For me, there is no better pie crust recipe than my mother's. When mom was a young book keeper, she rented a room from a woman from Germany who taught her how to bake pies and breads in the tradition of her homeland. The pastries mom learned to bake from Mrs. Creig (Gladdie's Pie Crust and Alfrey Rolls especially) are like no other.

Yield: Two double-crust pies, plus one single-crust pie

CRUST

4 cups all-purpose flour, sifted once with
1 teaspoon salt

1½ cups Crisco shortening, chilled
½ cup cold water
1 Tablespoon vinegar
1 large egg

- ♥ Using an electric mixer set with a dough hook; add the sifted flour and salt.
- ♥ Mix in the shortening cut into small cubes, and combine just until crumbly. Beat egg lightly with a fork.
- ♥ Combine the chilled water, egg and vinegar in separate bowl.
- ♥ Gradually add the "wet" ingredients to flour mixture while mixer is running and mix just until dough forms into a ball. Be careful to not over-mix dough or it will become stiff.

NOTES:
1) Always check liquid measurements at eye level for accuracy.
2) Pie dough can be made ahead and frozen for later use. Thaw dough in refrigerator.

Instructions (clockwise from top left):

Pat dough into a ball and place on a cool, hard and lightly floured surface for rolling;
Once rolled and shaped, fill pie plate by using rolling pin to hold dough while transferring;
Fit dough into pie plate and trim edges for uniformity;
Crimp, score and sprinkle - ready to bake

ROLLING & SHAPING PIE CRUST

For best results, roll pie dough on a cool hard surface and use heavy-gauge steel or aluminum pans. Glass or ceramic pans also work well, but should be baked at 25 degrees less heat than the recipe calls for.

BOTTOM CRUST – Divide pie dough and pat each piece into a flattened round. Place it on a lightly floured and clean countertop and sprinkle both sides with flour. Using a rolling pin dusted with flour, start in the center and roll lightly in all directions until round is large enough to cover bottom and sides of pie plate (approximately 1/8-inch thick and two inches greater than the diameter of pie pan).

147

Lift and turn the dough frequently to ensure it does not stick to the counter. Do not roll quite to the edge of dough until the last few turns. If the dough seems to be sticking, dust the counter with more flour.

Then, carefully roll the dough loosely over rolling pin, lift and place over pie plate. Unroll from one edge of plate to the other. Then use your hands to carefully adjust and center dough. Pat dough into all edges of pie plate, and then trim extra dough that is not uniform around outside rim.

At this point, chill the bottom crust, in the pie plate, to keep your baked bottom crust from being soggy.

OPEN-FACED PIES:
If you are making a single crust pie, crimp the edge of crust by using your thumb and forefinger. Press and pinch the dough together evenly at intervals around the rim. Build the rim up to about ¾-inch, then using your two fingers, press and pleat at intervals to make the dough stand up and create a scalloped edge.

Before baking an unfilled shell, be sure to prick the dough all across the bottom and along the sides. Shells should be baked at 375 degrees for 12 to 15 minutes, or until lightly browned. During the first 8 to 10 minutes of specified baking time, place a second, slightly smaller pie plate into the shell to help the crust hold its shape while baking. (See *Baking Pie Shells*, page 133.)

TOP CRUST – While your bottom shell is chilling, prepare the pie filling. Add filling to pie shell. Prepare second/top crust just like the first and roll onto the filled pie. Crimp the edges as instructed above, and then slice a cleaver design into top crust to create vents for steam to escape while baking.

BAKING:
Sprinkle the unbaked pie with sugar before baking. Use a pie crust shield for the first half of baking time. When baking fruit pies, it is advisable to place a pie shield sheet or aluminum foil beneath the pie plate to catch run-off juices.

For a crisp bottom crust, be sure to bake pies on the lowest rack of a thoroughly preheated oven.

Cookies

COOKIES

Brown Butter Shortbread

Cindy's Melt-in-Your-Mouth Shortbread

Front Porch Tea Cakes

Hazelnut Shortbread

Hello Dolly Bars

Holiday Sugar Cookies, Powdered Sugar Icing

Oatmeal Cookies, Sweet Coffee Glaze

Red Raspberry Chocolate Bars

Summer Sugar Cookies

Tart & Tangy Lemon Squares

Brown Butter Shortbread

I like to enjoy the crunchy outside of these cookies first, saving the chewy center for the last two bites! Caramelized butter & fresh lemon juice make this shortbread irresistible. Enjoy alone, or serve with coffee ice cream for an elegant yet simple dessert.

Yield: Two dozen cookies

Preparation, L to R: *Caramelized butter; Taking the Plunge; One-inch Balls; Score with Fork; Sprinkle with Sugar.*

1 cup unsalted butter
¾ teaspoon juice of fresh lemon
¾ cup granulated sugar
2 Tablespoons skim milk

2 teaspoons pure vanilla extract
2 cups all-purpose flour
1 teaspoon baking powder
½ teaspoon salt

- ♥ Prepare pan of ice water.
- ♥ Melt butter and continue cooking, stirring occasionally, until it smells like caramel and is almost ready to burn, approximately 10 minutes.
- ♥ When butter suddenly turns amber, plunge pan into ice water.
- ♥ Stir lemon juice into butter and let sit until solidified, approximately 20 minutes. Once butter is solid, Preheat oven to 300 degrees.
- ♥ Remove butter to large bowl with electric mixer and beat with sugar until fluffy. Beat in remaining ingredients, combining vanilla with milk and whisking flour with powder and salt before adding.
- ♥ Knead on a clean, lightly floured surface 10 to 12 times until smooth.
- ♥ In the palm of your hands, roll into small (1-inch diameter) balls.
- ♥ Place balls on ungreased baking sheet and flatten *slightly* with a fork, once horizontally and once vertically. Flattened balls should be no less than ½-inch in height to ensure a chewy center.
- ♥ Lightly sprinkle each cookie with sugar. Bake 20 to 25 minutes, or until edges are golden brown. Remove to wire rack to cool.

Cindy's Melt-in-your-Mouth Shortbread

My friend Cindy shares her family's iced shortbread cookies with my sister and me at our Christmas girl's lunch every year. The shortbread melts in your mouth and the pure sweetness of the icing make these cookies a delectable treat. Cindy always instructs us to share the cookies with our families, but we find them irresistible and usually eat our share of them in the car on the way home!

Yield: Two dozen cookies

SHORTBREAD

1 cup unsalted butter
2 cups all-purpose flour

2 heaping Tablespoons powdered sugar
1/8 teaspoon salt

- ♥ Preheat oven to 350 degrees.
- ♥ Combine all ingredients and mix with a pastry blender until crumbly.
- ♥ Then work the crumbs with your hands to form a ball of dough.
- ♥ Roll dough to ¼-inch thickness and cut into small round cookies.
- ♥ Bake for approximately 8 to 10 minutes, or until edges are lightly browned.

ICING

1 1-pound box powdered sugar
Water

Food coloring

- ♥ Mix powdered sugar with water until icing is thin yet spreadable.
- ♥ Add food coloring.
- ♥ Sprinkle iced cookies with decorative cookie candies.

Front Porch Tea Cakes

Yum, yum, yum! These cake-like cookies sprinkled with sugar are some of my favorites. Serve these treats the old fashioned way, on the front porch with friends and lemonade.

Yield: Approximately two dozen large rounds

1 cup unsalted butter
1½ cups granulated sugar
3 large eggs
4 cups all-purpose flour

2 teaspoons baking powder
1 teaspoon baking soda
½ teaspoon salt
¼ cup buttermilk
1 teaspoon almond extract

- ♥ Cream butter and sugar until light and fluffy. Add eggs and continue to cream.
- ♥ Whisk together dry ingredients (flour, powder, soda and salt) together. Mix dry ingredients with butter mixture alternately with buttermilk.
- ♥ Stir in extract and mix just until well combined. Chill dough for approximately **1 hour**.
- ♥ Preheat oven to 350 degrees.
- ♥ Roll out cookies and cut with a large, 2½-inch round cookie cutter. Place on greased cookie sheet. Sprinkle each cookie with granulated sugar. Bake for 15 minutes, or until lightly browned at edges.

Hazelnut Shortbread

The toasted hazelnuts add an almost earthy flavor to traditional buttery shortbread. Really good!

Yield: Two and one-half dozen cookies

1½ cups unsalted butter
1 cup powdered sugar
3 cups all-purpose flour
1 cup toasted hazelnuts, chopped

½ teaspoon salt
½ teaspoon pure vanilla extract
¼ cup granulated sugar

- ♥ Cream butter and powdered sugar until light and fluffy.
- ♥ Whisk flour and salt together. Blend flour, nuts and then vanilla with creamed mixture.
- ♥ Divide dough into three equal parts and wrap in waxed paper. Chill thoroughly (**about 1 hour**).
- ♥ Roll dough into ¾-inch thickness. Cut into hearts. Re-rolling and cutting until all dough has been used.
- ♥ Place cookies on an ungreased cookie sheet and pierce center of each cookie with a fork - twice to make a cross, and sprinkle with granulated sugar.
- ♥ Chill cookies, on cookie sheet for approximately 15 minutes.
- ♥ Preheat oven to 325 degrees.
- ♥ Bake for 20 minutes, or until shortbread just begins to brown lightly.

CHILLING THE DOUGH

When making cookies that are cut into shapes, it is important to chill the dough between the mixing and cutting to allow the shortening to solidify.

Skipping this step will result in dough that sticks to the counter and requires using more flour to roll out, *altering the flavor and texture of your cookies.*
I have found that dividing the dough into 2 to 3 batches before chilling allows you to work with a smaller amount of dough while cutting and keeps the dough cool and easy to work with.

Hello Dolly Bars

These bar cookies are a real treat for my husband and satisfy his sweet tooth! Whenever we visit his parents they are waiting in the kitchen for his arrival.

Yield: Approximately two dozen squares

½ cup unsalted butter
1 cup buttery crackers, crushed
1 6-ounce package milk chocolate chips

1 6-ounce can Angel Flake coconut
1 cup pecans, chopped
1 cup condensed milk

- ♥ Preheat oven to 325 degrees.
- ♥ Melt butter in an oblong baking dish.
- ♥ Layer remaining ingredients in the following order: Crushed crackers, chocolate chips, coconut, and pecans. Pour milk evenly over all.
- ♥ Bake for 30 minutes. Cool, cover and refrigerate overnight. Cut into squares.

Holiday Sugar Cookies with Powdered Sugar Icing

These cookies are a holiday tradition on both Easter and Christmas, and can be adapted to any holiday or special occasion, depending on the cookie cutters used and choice of icing colors. These delicious sugar cookies are soft in the middle, and by sifting the powdered sugar, yield a wonderful crispy edge. I recommend baking a double recipe because these really go fast!

Yield: Three dozen cookies

	DOUBLE RECIPE
1½ cups powdered sugar, sifted	3 cups powdered sugar, sifted
1 cup unsalted butter, softened	2 cup unsalted butter, softened
1 large egg	2 large eggs
1 teaspoon pure vanilla extract	2 teaspoons pure vanilla extract
½ teaspoon almond extract	1 teaspoon almond extract
2½ cups all-purpose flour	5 cups all-purpose flour
1 teaspoon baking soda	2 teaspoons baking soda
1 teaspoon cream of tartar	2 teaspoons cream of tartar

- ♥ In a large bowl with electric mixer at medium speed, cream powdered sugar and butter until light and fluffy. Add egg with vanilla and almond extracts and continue to cream.
- ♥ Sift the dry ingredients together onto a sheet of waxed paper, and then gradually add to creamed mixture one large spoonful at a time, working swiftly to avoid over-mixing, or dough will be tough.
  Scrape sides of bowl throughout mixing process to ensure even distribution of ingredients.
- ♥ Divide dough into three equal parts, wrap in waxed paper and refrigerate for **3 to 4 hours**.
- ♥ Preheat oven to 350 degrees.
- ♥ On a clean, lightly floured surface with lightly floured rolling pin, roll dough (one part at a time) to ¼-inch thick. Cut with cookie cutters, as appropriate to holiday, and place on baking sheets. Reroll trimmings and cut more cookies, using care to handle dough as little as possible.

Bake 7 to 8 minutes on ungreased cookie sheet until lightly browned yet soft in the middle. Remove to wire rack and ice when cool.

♥ Sprinkle lightly with sugar while icing is still in liquid form.

♥ Store in an airtight container up to 4 days.

NOTE: Cookies can be baked, iced and frozen up to one month.
To freeze or store iced cookies, place on cookie sheet and freeze for one hour before placing into tins. This will allow icing to solidify and avoid sticking.

Powdered Sugar Icing

Yield: Enough icing for a single cookie recipe.

1 1-pound box powdered sugar　　　**1 teaspoon extract** (See notes below)
1 Tablespoon milk　　　**Food coloring** (See notes below)

♥ Sift powdered sugar to avoid lumps in icing. Then whisk with milk until smooth and creamy. Add milk gradually to ensure desired consistency. For a lighter icing, add more milk.

♥ Combine first three ingredients and stir until smooth.

♥ Add a small drop of food coloring to start, and additional drops until desired color. *I find pale/pastel icing colors much more appetizing, and 1 to 2 drops of color are plenty.*

USING EXTRACTS WITH FOOD COLORING

Try dividing the icing into four small bowls before adding ¼ teaspoon extract and 1 small drop of color to the sugar and milk in each bowl. Then match different extracts with different food coloring for a subtle surprise in each bite.

For example:

First bowl: *Peppermint extract with blue food coloring*
Second bowl: *Almond extract with green food coloring*
Third bowl: *Coconut extract with yellow food coloring*
Fourth bowl: *Lemon or orange extract with red food coloring*

Oatmeal Cookies with Sweet Coffee Glaze

These sugary treats have a coffee glaze drizzled over the warm cookies.

Yield: Approximately three dozen cookies

COOKIES

½ cup butter, softened
½ cup Crisco shortening
1 cup packed brown sugar
1 cup granulated sugar
2 large eggs
1½ teaspoons pure vanilla extract

1¾ cups all-purpose flour
1 teaspoon baking soda
1 teaspoon salt
3 cups old fashioned rolled oats (not instant)
½ cup raisins, plumped

- ♥ Preheat oven to 375 degrees. Plump raisins in ½ cup hot coffee for 20 to 30 minutes, or until soft and supple.
- ♥ Cream butter and Crisco with sugars until light and fluffy. Add eggs and continue to cream. Add vanilla.
- ♥ Whisk dry ingredients (flour, soda and salt) together. Mix dry ingredients with butter mixture. Add oatmeal; mix. Fold in raisins.
- ♥ Scoop dough into heaping Tablespoons and place on ungreased cookie sheets. Bake 8 to 10 minutes, or until golden brown with crisp edges.
- ♥ Remove cookies to a cooling rack, with waxed paper underneath, as soon as they are baked. Drizzled warm glaze over warm cookies.
- ♥ Allow to cool.

GLAZE

2 Tablespoons butter
2 Tablespoons strong brewed coffee
1 teaspoon pure vanilla extract

1 teaspoon cinnamon
1 cup powdered sugar

- ♥ Melt butter. Whisk in coffee, vanilla and cinnamon. Sift powdered sugar into butter-coffee mixture and whisk to combine.
- ♥ Drizzle while still warm over cookies. Reheat glaze as necessary.

Red Raspberry-Chocolate Bars

I love these bar cookies. The crust is thick and chewy and the topping is berry sweet and chocolaty. This recipe is involved, but worth the time.

Yield: Six dozen bite-sized bars

¼ cup shelled whole hazelnuts, chopped
¼ cup slivered blanched almonds
2½ cups all-purpose flour
½ teaspoon baking powder
¼ teaspoon salt
½ cup unsalted butter, slightly softened

1/3 cup plus 2 Tablespoons granulated sugar
3 large eggs
1 Tablespoon orange juice, freshly squeezed
10 ounces *red* raspberry jelly
2½ ounces semisweet chocolate

- ♥ Preheated oven to 325 degrees.
- ♥ In a shallow baking pan, toast hazelnuts 16 to 18 minutes, or until hulls begin to loosen and nuts are slightly colored and fragrant. Remove from oven and set aside to cool. When nuts are cool enough to handle, remove hulls by vigorously rubbing a handful at a time in a clean dish towel. (Some skin may remain on hazelnuts, but they should be free of the bitter hull.
- ♥ Spread the almonds in a separate baking dish and toast in a preheated 325 degree oven for 5 minutes. Remove from the oven and cool completely. Combine nuts and chop moderately fine.
- ♥ Sift together flour, baking powder and salt onto a sheet of waxed paper. Set aside.
- ♥ In a large mixing bowl, beat butter and sugar until fluffy.
  Add **2 of the eggs** and the orange juice and beat until well blended.
- ♥ Stir in **half of the dry** ingredients and **1/3 cup** of the chopped nuts. (Reserve remaining nuts to decorate cookies.)
- ♥ Stir remaining dry ingredients and mix until dough begins to hold together. Divide dough into thirds and place each third on a large sheet of waxed paper. Using your hands, roll each wrapped dough section into a log 11-inches long.

♥ Transfer logs to a baking sheet lightly coated with cooking spray, spacing them as far apart from one another as possible.
Use the sides of your hand to form a deep trough, about 1½-inches wide, down the center. (Be sure the trough has a rim all the way around it to keep jelly from running.)

♥ Place remaining egg in a small bowl and beat with one Tablespoon water until well combined. Brush tops and sides of each log with egg mixture. Bake in the center of preheated 325 degree oven for 9 minutes. Remove from oven.

♥ Lightly brush logs again with egg mixture. (You will only use about 1/3 of this mixture). Spoon about 2½ Tablespoons of the jelly evenly along the indentation of each log; lightly sprinkle logs with half of remaining chopped nuts, reserving second half for decoration.

♥ Return logs to oven and bake 11 to 13 minutes longer, or until dough browned and the jelly is bubbly. Remove from the oven and let stand 15 minutes. Transfer to wire racks set over waxed paper.

♥ In top of a double boiler, combine chocolates with remaining 2 Tablespoons of butter and carefully stir until smooth. Remove from heat. *Be sure no moisture gets into the chocolate, or otherwise it will "tighten."* If this happens, smooth it out with 2 teaspoons of Crisco shortening.

♥ Drizzle chocolate over logs, sprinkle with remaining nuts, and let stand until completely cooled.

♥ Transfer logs to cutting board. Using a long, sharp knife, slice each log lengthwise and then into 12 to 13 slices crosswise. Store in an airtight container up to 4 days.

NOTE: Logs can be frozen whole up to one month, then thawed and sliced before serving. To freeze logs, place on cookie sheet and freeze for one hour before wrapping and storing. This will avoid distorting the chocolate drizzles.

Summer Sugar Cookies

These minty sugar cookies are an unusual summer treat. Fresh mint is a must!

Yield: Three dozen flower-shaped cookies

1 cup unsalted butter, softened
1¼ cups granulated sugar
1 large egg
½ cup sour cream
¼ teaspoon mint extract
¼ cup fresh mint leaves, minced

4 cups all-purpose flour
1 teaspoon baking powder
½ teaspoon baking soda
¼ teaspoon salt
Sugar
Un-blanched almond slices

- ♥ In a large bowl with electric mixer at medium speed, beat butter, sugar and egg until light and fluffy. At low speed, beat in sour cream and mint extract until smooth. Mix in mint leaves.
- ♥ Gradually beat in 2 cups flour that has been whisked together with baking powder, soda and salt until well combined. With a spoon, fold in enough remaining flour to form a stiff dough, being careful to not over mix.
- ♥ Divide dough into four equal parts; wrap in waxed paper and refrigerate **1 to 2 hours**.
- ♥ Preheat oven to 375 degrees. Lightly grease three cookie sheets.
- ♥ On a clean, lightly floured surface, roll dough (one part at a time) to ¼-inch thick. With 2 to 3-inch flower-shaped cookie cutter, cut out cookies and place on baking sheet lightly coated with cooking spray.
- ♥ Reroll trimmings and cut more cookies, using care to avoid over handling cookie dough. Roll dough evenly to ensure cookies bake evenly. Space cookies with approximately one inch between each cookie and the sides of your pans, as they will expand while baking.
- ♥ Lightly sprinkle each cookie with sugar, and gently press an almond slice in the center of each. Bake 8 to 10 minutes, or until golden brown. Remove to wire rack to cool. Store in an airtight container up to 4 days.

HOW TO ROLL AND BAKE
PERFECT COOKIES

Always chill the dough for rolled cookies as directed. Solidifying the batter will ensure your dough does not stick to your countertop when rolled out. If your dough still seems sticky after chilling, sprinkle the counter and rolling pin with a bit more flour.

Roll the dough to a minimum ¼-inch thickness and then cut into shapes, using either cookie cutters or the rim of a glass. After the shaped cookies have been cut out, gather up the scraps, put them together handling dough as little as possible, and roll or pat them out again to make more cookies.

Always bake cookies in a preheated oven, and only bake one sheet at a time (unless using a convection oven). Watch cookies carefully while baking. Some thinner cookies especially, can take as little as 5 minutes to brown. Baking time also varies with ovens, *so be sure to set your timer for less time than the recipe calls for,* check cookies half way through and rotate pan(s), then cook for more time if necessary. Chewy cookies should be baked slightly less time and crisp cookies more, depending on personal preference.

Let cookie sheets cool before adding another batch to them or the second batch may not hold its shape. Remove cookie to cooling rack as soon as they are cool enough to handle. If cookies remain on sheets too long and begin to stick to pans, just pop them in the oven for a few minutes to soften them, and then try removing again.

Do not stack cookies or store them until they have cooled completely, or they will not be crisp. When freezing cookies, place sheets of waxed paper between the rows to prevent sticking. When freezing cookies that have been iced, drizzled with chocolate or glazed, freeze cookies on a sheet first and allow the icing to freeze and set in place. Otherwise, the icing will stick to your paper and come off the cookies as you unpack them.

Tart & Tangy Lemon Squares

These Lemon Squares are sweet and tart and perfect any time of year.

Yield: Eighteen medium-sized squares

SHORTBREAD CRUST

1¾ cups all-purpose flour
2/3 cup powdered sugar, plus more
for sifting on top

¼ cup cornstarch
¾ teaspoon salt
12 Tablespoons cool butter

- ♥ Cut butter into 1-inch pieces. Line a 9 x 13-inch baking pan with parchment paper. Dot with butter, then lay a second piece of paper crosswise over it.
- ♥ Combine the flour, powdered sugar, cornstarch and salt in a food processor. Piece by piece, add the cool butter, working quickly to ensure the butter does not melt. Process 8 to 10 seconds, or until the mixture resembles a coarse meal.
- ♥ Transfer the crust mixture into the prepared pan and press (with your hands) until the dough covers the pan in an even layer with about ½- inch rim up the sides of the pan. Refrigerate for **20 to 30 minutes**.
- ♥ Preheat oven to 350 degrees and place oven rack in middle position.
- ♥ Bake for 15 to 20 minutes, or until golden brown.

LEMON FILLING

4 large eggs
1 1/3 cups granulated sugar
3 Tablespoons all-purpose flour
Rind of 2 lemons, grated

Juice of 3 large lemons
1/3 cup milk
1/8 teaspoon salt

- ♥ Reduce oven temperature to 325 degrees.
- ♥ Whisk together the eggs, sugar and flour in a medium bowl. Stir in the lemon zest, juice and milk. Pour the filling onto the warm crust (Be sure the crust is still warm so the filling can incorporate into the top layers of shortbread crust). Bake for 18 to 20 minutes, or until the filling sets and feels slightly firm to the touch. Cool bars to room temperature. Lightly sift powdered sugar over squares. Remove to a cutting board and cut into squares with a pizza cutter.

163

BAKING TIPS

As with cakes, it is best to have all ingredients at room temperature before you begin to bake cookies. Use all-purpose flour, unless otherwise indicated.

It is not necessary to sift flour when baking cookies unless specified in recipe instructions. However, I do recommend always whisking flour with salt, soda and/or powder to ensure all is thoroughly combined. Skipping this step can result in a bite of cookie that is overly salty or bitter.

Use sturdy cookie sheets that are the right size for your oven, with room for air to circulate around each sheet. Avoid using pans with a high side for baking cookies (sides deflect heat and cookies will be misshapen).

When cookie dough contains a good deal of butter, it is not necessary to grease the sheets. To use butter to grease you sheets, use the unwrapped paper from a stick of butter.

There is no need to wash sheets between batches of cookies, just scrape off any crumbs and continue using until all the batter has been baked.

164

The *Art* of Entertaining

THE ART OF ENTERTAINING

Pre-Work

A Sensory Experience

Setting the Table

Food & Wine Pairing

Edible Flowers & Herbs

Candied Flowers

Chilling with Style

Tussie Mussies

Tricks of the Trade

The Art of Entertaining

Entertaining family and friends is fun, and made easy via the pre-work.

Once the invitation has been issued, plan your menu, wines and décor, then backtrack. Consider each step of each task and determine how much can be done ahead of time. The more pre-work you complete before the guests arrive, the more you will be able to enjoy the party.

Consider what aspects of your meal might be prepared early, like the desert. Then consider what parts will take the longest and determine what time the preparation should start. If there are unfamiliar techniques involved, immerse yourself in the material to ensure an understanding before you begin.

Take the time to do as much in advance as you possibly can, leaving only the last minute heat-and-eat tasks for the actual event, then enjoy the party!

The Pre-Work

Throughout this cookbook, I have noted when dishes can be made ahead, or partially completed to make entertaining fun for the cook as well. I suggest making a timeline to organize when entertaining. Below is a sample timeline for Thanksgiving Dinner.

Menu

Black-eyed Susans
Secret Roast Turkey
Cornbread Dressing, Mashed Potatoes and Scrumptious Pan Gravy
Green Beans with Almonds
Holiday Pie

One month before the party

Make the Black-Eyed Susans and freeze.

One week before the party

Assemble dressing and freeze (unbaked).

Two days before

Set the table; arrange centerpiece; make place cards.
Make pie crust; refrigerate. Chill wine.

One day before

Brine Turkey; refrigerate.
Prepare Pan Gravy through first steps to straining of fat.
Toast almonds; store in air tight container.
Wash/snap beans & refrigerate in damp paper towel in sealed container.
Prepare vegetables for roasting with turkey (Wrap in damp paper towels and refrigerate to avoid discoloring.)

Early the day of your party

Add fresh flowers to your centerpiece.
Assemble pie and bake. Assemble turkey and roast.
Peel potatoes and refrigerate wrapped in damp paper toweling.
Remove cornbread and Susans from freezer.

One hour before serving

Bake and serve black-eyed Susans with beverage of choice. Bake cornbread.

One half hour before serving

Cook and mash potatoes. Cook beans. Finish gravy.

Just before serving

Fill water and wine glasses.
Carve turkey and arrange on a platter.
Add almonds to beans and season.

A Sensory Experience

Eating is a sensory experience. When planning your menu remember that the sensory experience is as important as the palatable.

Two tips to always remember:

1) *Make sure your meal has both a hot and cold dish.*
   This can be as simple as a cold salad with a hot fried egg. A bite of warmth in an otherwise cold meal enhances the sensory experience.

2) *Be mindful of the color palate.*
   Consider the colors of each dish as you plan your menu, and avoid meals that are all one shade. For example, if serving fried chicken and mashed potatoes (gold and cream), avoid carrots or a vegetable in the same color family. You can jazz up your plate of fried chicken, and create a more appetizing presentation, with a bright green vegetable.

   Couple these tips with a pretty table and your family and friends will be reminded of how much they are loved.

SUBSTITUTIONS

Many items can be substituted in the kitchen, or made from other ingredients. For example, you can make cake flour from all-purpose flour and buttermilk from sweet milk in just a few simple steps.

Throughout this cookbook, I have noted secrets to key substitutions, along with cooking tips from how to handle vegetables to how to ice a cake. Be sure to review tips dispersed throughout this publication as they are inserted as they apply to recipes.

Setting the Table

The dining experience today is often informal and the etiquette of setting a proper table dismissed as too "Victorian." In fact, my grandmother would have fainted at all the boldness of the anything-goes approach used in the 21st-century. In her world, hard and fast rules were dutifully applied and conservative was the name of the game.

My style as a hostess is to respect the basic rules for setting a table while expressing my creativity by combining and coordinating patterns and colors. My mantra is that every table, no matter how informal, should be laid with care and attention to detail. Pretty settings help make the food look better and make guests feel that an effort has been made on their behalf. On page 178, you will find a sampling of ideas to get your creative juices flowing when designing your table scapes. Memorize the basics outlined below, and then enjoy feeding your creativity - as well as family and friends!

FLATWARE

At left: *A traditional place setting with a full service of matching china, silver & stemware including linens, a place card & a salt- pepper set for each guest.*

- ♥ Place flatware one inch from the edge of table at place settings that are equidistant from one another on the table. The base of all flatware should align evenly across the bottom of each place setting.
- ♥ Set your table with whatever silver is needed for the meal. Traditionally, that needed first is placed farthest right and left of the plate.
- ♥ The forks are usually two, for salad and meat; occasionally one more for the appetizer, but never more than three beside the plate at once.

170

- The dessert fork and spoon, when part of the setting, are placed above the plate. The dessert spoon is placed above the fork. The spoon handle points to the right, the fork handle the left.
- The salad fork is placed to the outside of the meat fork, only when the salad is served as a first course. (If only one course is being served, only provide one fork.)
- The knife is usually limited to one – unless an appetizer is served. Then provide one knife for the appetizer, and one for the meat. If salad is to be served with cheese, a salad knife is needed.
- Spoons are on the table, to the right of the knives.
- The blade of the knife faces the plate.

NAPKINS

At Left: *A simple summer setting with seashells.*

- The napkin may be placed on the plate, unless the first course is in place, in which case it is to the left of the forks.

PLATES

At Left: *Fall table of china, pottery, mixed stemware & creative napkin ring.*

♥   If you want to be formal, you should use a salad plate. If you do not have a maid or wait staff (as many do not any more) then either preset the salad on its plate, or dispense with a salad plate entirely. The exception to this rule would be if your main course is something very runny or gooey. Then a separate salad plate is recommended regardless.

♥   Consider if your dinner plate is large enough for the meal you are planning. If your meat, salad, vegetable and roll are all on one plate, it should be twelve inches in diameter. Otherwise, give guests a smaller plate for either the salad and/or bread or roll.

♥   If coffee is to be served, place a cup and saucer to the right of the dinner plate with a spoon placed on each saucer.

BUTTER PLATES

♥   If you wish to have butter on the table, to pass around family style, make it look pretty by placing it on an earthenware or porcelain plate, with a butter knife.
The same applies for presenting salt and pepper, if individual sets cannot be provided at place settings.

♥   If you are serving bread or rolls, I recommend using a butter plate, placed at upper left side of setting beside forks. Butter plates and knives are used with the butter knife placed across the top of the plates, handle toward the user.

♥   A pat or round of butter can also be placed on each butter plate and alleviate the need for passing.

GLASSES

At Left: *A mixed setting with "found" centerpiece.*

♥ Glasses may be placed on a diagonal, starting with the water glass above the knife, and leading to the lower left.

♥ The white wine glass is used for the first course. The middle, red-wine glass, is used during the remaining courses.

♥ The wineglass should be filled about halfway, just to the point where the glass (shape) breaks.

♥ Pouring the wines: When the guests are seated, the host should walk around the table, serving the woman honored guest on his right first, and serving everyone else around the table clockwise.

SALT & PEPPER

♥ At a large table a salt and pepper set should be placed for every two guests.

CENTERPIECES

♥ Centerpieces and table decorations should be low enough for all guests to be seen.

CANDLESTICKS

- ♥ Candlesticks on the luncheon table do not belong.
- ♥ Candlesticks, when used for dinner, should always be lit.
- ♥ Candles should be above eye level to avoid glare in guests' eyes.

MENU CARDS & PLACE CARDS

At Left: *A holiday table with whimsy.*

- ♥ Menu cards are a fun way to make your evening elegant and showcase the meal. Be sure to make one for each guest. Approximately 4½ x 6½-inches is a good size.
- ♥ Place the date at the upper right and "Dinner" or "Lunch" in the upper center.
- ♥ If you are an accomplished hostess, it is fun to write your menus in English, French and/or Italian.
- ♥ Leave a bit of space between courses so that your guests will know how the meal is being served.
- ♥ If your party is a special celebration, indicate this on the top of card.

- ♥ Place cards are used for formal dinner parties and display only the guest's name. Place cards allow guests to be strategically placed around the table to ensure everyone enjoys the conversation and celebration.
- ♥ If you have guests with limited mobility, place cards also ensure these friends have easy access to and from the table.

GRATITUDE

- ♥ Entertaining takes a good deal of effort. One should always send a thank-you note after having dinner or lunch in someone's home.

Food & Wine Pairing

Pairing food with wine can seem intimidating, but can be as simplistic as matching color and considering weight.

Here are a few easy tips to help you get started.

1) *Match color with color. Poultry and pork are best served with white wine. Beef and lamb work better with reds.*

2) *Consider weight. If your dish includes a rich white sauce, choose a rich white wine. If beef is served with a sauce, use a light red. If your beef has a very flavorful sauce, then serve a more full-bodied red wine.*

Other easy tips to remember:

- ♥ *Serve chianti with tomato sauce*
- ♥ *Goat cheese with sauvignon blanc*
- ♥ *Bordeaux with steak or beef*
- ♥ *Oysters with champagne*
- ♥ *Port with Stilton cheese*
- ♥ *Meat and fruit with a German Riesling*

Guidelines

- ♥ Acid neutralizes acid.

  When a vinaigrette salad dressing is paired with a rich, buttery chardonnay the flavors will neutralize each other. Instead, use a crisp sauvignon blanc with anything vinegar-based so the flavors can complement one another.

- ♥ Light with light.

  When serving lighter cheeses, choose a light red or white wine.

- ♥ Fuller with fuller.

  When serving a fuller cheese, choose a fuller wine.

- ♥ Salt neutralizes tannin.

  A Cabernet wine can dominate your mouth. However a few bites of something very salty, like a tortilla chip, will remove the wine's flavor completely. If you have chosen a lovely cab for your meal, be mindful of the salt or your thoughtful wine selection will be for naught.

- ♥ Dessert wines must be sweeter than the dessert.

- ♥ Match the region.

  The best pairing is often found by choosing a wine from the same region that your food has originated from.

Utilizing Flowers in Creative Ways

*Nothing brings more joy to the table scape than fresh flowers. I love using fresh, in-season blossoms as a centerpiece, and using flowers and herbs to decorate baked goods and entrées. When using flowers in creative ways be sure to learn which varieties are safe to consume. **Not all flowers are edible, and plants should not be consumed if they've been sprayed with pesticide.***

Edible Flowers & Herbs

Flowers Safe to Consume		
Bachelor's button	Honeysuckle	Peony
Begonia	Jasmine	Phlox
Carnations	Johnny Jump-ups	Rose
Chrysanthemum	Lavender	Scented geraniums
Clover	Lilac	Snapdragon
Dandelion	Marigold	Sunflower
Day Lilies	Nasturtium	Squash
Hardy Hibiscus	Okra	Tulip petals
Hollyhock	Pansy	Violet

Edible Herb Blossoms			
Basil	Garlic	Mint	Rosemary
Chives	Lemon Verbena	Onions	Sage
Fennel	Marjoram	Oregano	Thyme

Incorporate flowers that are at their peak of bloom and collect them in the early part of the day. Try to avoid unopened blossoms as they can be bitter.

Candied Flowers

Each spring I candy a batch of the wild violets that grow in profusion around our home. Roses are also pretty candied, and both can be used to garnish cakes and other desserts.

1 cup of fresh safe-to-consume flowers or flower petals, rinsed in cool water and allowed to air-dry naturally on paper towels
1 egg white, beaten lightly until foamy
½ cup superfine sugar
1 small, clean artist's paintbrush, suitable for detailed work
Toothpicks, enough for each flower
Styrofoam board, approximately 18 x 18-inches and 1-inch thick.

- ♥ Carefully spear each flower with a toothpick on the underside of blossom. Penetrate center just far enough to hold in place. (Not necessary when using petals only)
- ♥ Using your paint brush lightly coat the entire surface of each petal, top and bottom, with a thin coating of egg white.
- ♥ While petals are still moist, with your fingers, lightly sprinkle the sugar on all surfaces. Gently swirl pick between your fingers to shake off excess sugar. Insert toothpick into Styrofoam board so that air can circulate around all sides of flower and it can dry naturally. Do not try to reuse sugar; it will be too moist to cover evenly.
- ♥ Allow flowers to dry completely, uncovered, before using; approximately 4 to 8 hours, depending on humidity. Use flowers to garnish baked goods at first opportunity for best results.
- ♥ *Flowers can be stored in air-tight container between layers of waxed paper for up to one month before losing their color.*

HOW TO MAKE SUPERFINE SUGAR

If you do not have superfine sugar in your pantry, you can easily make it.
Simply pulse granulated sugar in a blender until it becomes powder-like in texture. Do not try to substitute granulated sugar for superfine.

Chilling with Style

Pansies and/or violets   **Mint leaves**
Rose petals   **Ice cube trays**

- ♥ Place rinsed pansies, rose petals and mint leaves at the bottom of each compartment of filled ice-cube trays.
- ♥ Place in the freezer and allow water to freeze.
- ♥ In lieu of an ice bucket, choose a pretty bowl large enough to chill a bottle of wine.
- ♥ When the cubes are set, fill the bowl, and add a bottle of lemonade, wine or champagne.
- ♥ Chill *elegantly* until ready to serve!

TEN IDEAS FOR CREATIVE TABLES
Use these ideas to get your own creativity flowing!

Use memorabilia from far-away places when dining with fellow travelers.

Use sand dollars as place cards (write names on dollars) for a beach party.

Stuff and spray colorful paper napkins from glassware on any occasion.

Place julep cups filled with roses at each place setting on Derby Day.

Fill a window box with seasonal blossoms for a summery centerpiece.

Serve salt and pepper from oyster half shells to contrast formal china.

Craft napkin rings from rolls of firecrackers on the Fourth of July.

Place palm branches under place settings and centerpiece for Easter.

Make votive(s) from small pumpkins and gourds for Thanksgiving.

Use family heirlooms like tiny shoes and photos when hosting a baby shower.

Tussie Mussies

From the earliest times Tussie Mussies have been associated with wedding ritual, and were a widespread Victorian tradition for courtship. Created with herbs and flowers, each with their own story to tell, these precious individualized bouquets convey your best wishes. As my friend Rosemary would say, giving a Tussie Mussie to someone is like presenting her with a love letter. The next time you host a bridal shower, consider gifting the bride with a Tussie Mussie for her trousseau.

This "recipe" is for a Tussie Mussie received from Rosemary as a bride-to-be:

ROSE – Symbolizing beauty, youth and love

ROSEMARY – For devotion and loyalty, as well as remembrance

SAGE – To ensure domestic virtues

ARTIMESIA – The Chinese symbol for dignity

BORAGE LEAVES – For courage

MONEY PLANT – Ensures money in your pocket

LAVENDER – For purity and cleanliness

STRAWFLOWER and/or COREOPSIS – To say, "Always Yours"

BRIDE'S BUTTONS – For loyal love

CARAWAY – To call a straying husband back to hearth and home (should you ever need it)

MUGWORT – To keep witches away (in the hard-to imagine possibility that your mother-in-law acts like one)

YELLOW JASMINE (vine) – For genius (added for my husband Todd)

- ♥ Arrange all foliage into a small bouquet.
- ♥ Bind with affection, best wishes, a doily and a ribbon tied in a bow.

179

OTHER SYMBOLIC HERBS & FLOWERS

2 MINITURE ROSES – Symbolizes two sweethearts

PARSLEY – To "perk" the appetite

OREGANO – A cure for baldness

BASIL – To procure a cheerful and merry heart

MINT – To stir desire

VIOLET (flower and leaves) – The ancient flowers of love and

faithfulness

CHIVE – A valuable antidote (for what ails you)

CARNATION (flower and leaves) – Symbolic of the engagement of

hearts, minds and hands

PANSEY – The happy "face"

PHLOX (flower and leaves) - Stateliness

Developing Good Cooking Habits

Before you start your mixer or turn on the stove, read through your recipes from start to finish. Think about what you are supposed to be doing and why. Consider the time it will take and give yourself a bit of leeway so you don't get flustered. Then, set all of your ingredients out on the counter to ensure you have what is called for. There's nothing worse than getting half way through a recipe to discover you are missing a key ingredient.

The secret to a great meal is to time all dishes to finish cooking at same time. This way you and your guests will enjoy each dish as it was meant to be served.

When planning your menu, consider what is in season and what is on special in the market. Ingredients always taste better when they are at their peak of freshness. Don't skimp on essentials like extra-virgin/good quality olive oil, pure vanilla extract, fresh herbs and the like. Be flexible when planning your menus and prepare dishes that take advantage of nature's natural timetable.

Other Tips

- *Plan more complicated dishes for the weekend when you have more time.*
- *Before going to the market, plan 2 to 4 meals and make a list of needed ingredients. Busy weeknights are easier when you know what's for dinner before you arrive home and are mentally prepared to begin cooking.*
- *Build a pantry that is chocked full of the "staples." This will also make preparing home-cooked and healthy meals easier and doable.*

In several of my recipes, I suggest making a double batch or recipe and freezing the second half for a rainy day. It is comforting to have meals ready in the freezer and is a nice treat when you know you'll be home late or come home tired. Likewise, be creative with leftovers. Find ways to re-make them slightly or add something fresh to last night's entrée rather than simply heating up the same exact meal in the microwave (it never tastes quite as good).

For example:

If on Monday night you are serving grilled chicken breasts, corn on the cob and Swiss chards with leeks, prepare an extra breast and ear of corn.

On Tuesday night, with less than ten minutes of active cooking time, you can have a completely different meal.

Start by tossing a couple potatoes in the oven to bake, and then about 45 minutes later, steam some fresh asparagus. Then re-heat the leftover chicken breast and ear of corn, in the oven on a cookie sheet, with the potatoes during the last fifteen minutes of baking time. Cut the kernels from the corn cob, and mound across the center of whole asparagus spears. Serve with the warm chicken breast and potatoes.

Kitchen Essentials

Over time, try to collect kitchen essentials. Treat yourself to good cake pans and a cooling rack as your budget allows, for example. Purchase these items gradually as you need them to prepare new recipes, and replace them as necessary. Before you know it, you kitchen will be well stocked.

KITCHEN STAPLES

Baking Powder, Baking Soda, beans, bouillon cubes, fresh herbs, homemade bread crumbs, butter, nuts, chocolate (a variety, including cocoa), coconut, cream and milk, Cream of Tartar, eggs, Crisco shortening, flour (all-purpose and cake), fresh garlic, oils (a variety, along with olive oil), onions, pasta, preserves, rice, sour cream, sugar (granulated, brown and powdered), syrup, cornstarch, vinegar, wines and liquors, yeast and pure vanilla extract.

Other staples include plastic containers, aluminum foil, plastic wrap, plastic baggies, waxed paper and parchment paper, and paper towels.

ESSENTIAL KITCHEN EQUIPMENT

Measuring cups (one set for wet ingredients and one for dry), measuring spoons, meat thermometer and candy/frying thermometer, Kitchen timer (in addition to the one on your stove), mixing bowls, chopping board, good knives (these are expensive and can be collected one at a time if necessary), knife sharpener, kitchen shears and twine, vegetable parer, can opener, pepper grinder, funnel, nut grinder, grater, colander, strainer, salad spinner.

I also recommend a grapefruit knife, melon baller, zester, mortar and pestle, meat pounder, scales.

For cooking you'll need pots/skillets/pans, wooden spoons, rubber spatulas, metal utensils such as slotted spoons, tongs, whisks, skewers, and basting brushes (one for cooking and one for baking) and a pizza brick.

For baking you'll need a good quality, heavy duty standing electric mixer (such as Kitchen Aid), hand mixer, pastry blender, rolling pin, flour sifter, cake pans, loaf pans, Bundt pan, cookie sheets, jelly roll pan, muffin tins, pie pans, a pie crust shield, at least one cooling rack, and a food processor and/or blender.

I also recommend a pastry scrapper, pastry/biscuit/cookie cutters, pizza cutter, spring form pan, and small tart tins.

Glossary of Cooking Terms

A-B

Al Dente – To briefly cook (pasta) just long enough to be firm to the bite and almost tender; slightly undercooked. In Italian, this means, "To the tooth."

Baguette – A long, thin loaf of French bread.

Bake – To cook by dry heat in an oven.

Baste – To moisten, especially meats, with pan drippings or melted butter, during the cooking time.

Beat – To mix ingredients by vigorously stirring with an electric mixer.

Blanch – Typically used with vegetables and fruit – To immerse briefly into boiling water to inactivate enzymes, loosen skin or soak away excess salt.

Blend – To combine two or more ingredients, one being liquid or soft, to quickly produce a mixture of uniform consistency.

Boil – To heat liquid until bubbly (approximately 212 degrees for boiling water).

Braise – A method of cooking meats, covered in a small amount of liquid.

Broil – To cook by direct exposure to intense heat, such as a flame or heating unit at top of oven.

C

Caramelize – The process of melting sugar until golden brown. This can be done in a heavy pan over a low heat (stirring constantly) or atop a cookie or cake while it is baking.

Chiffonade – To shred with a fast, quick pass of the knife, ensuring the flavor is not left on the cutting board. Often used with herbs.

Chill – To cool in the refrigerator or in ice.

Cream – To blend butter or shortening with a granulated sugar or crushed ingredient until soft and creamy (or light and fluffy).

Crème Frâiche – Fresh, cold cream.

Crimp – A method of sealing the edges of double-crusted pies by using index finger of one hand to push the inner edge out while pinching the outer edge in with the thumb and index finger of other hand to make a little, classic scallop edge.

Crudité – Traditional French appetizers consisting of sliced or whole raw vegetables which are sometimes dipped in vinaigrette or other dipping sauce. Crudités often include celery sticks, carrot sticks, bell pepper strips, broccoli, green beans and asparagus spears; sometimes olives.

Cube – To chop into small squares, approximately ½-inch.

Curdle – To congeal milk or milk fat until soft lumps or curds are formed.

Cut in – To disperse solid shortening into dry ingredients with a pastry blender or knife. The finished texture resembles coarse meal and looks crumbly.

D

Deglaze – To heat a liquid such as stock or wine in the pan in which meat has been cooked. When mixed with pan drippings, the liquid forms a flavorful gravy or sauce base.

Dice – To cut into small squares, approximately 1/8-inch.

Dissolve – To thoroughly mix a granular substance with a liquid.

Dollop – To lump or blob a small quantity.

Dredge – To coat with flour or bread crumbs.

Drizzle – To lightly sprinkle in controlled stream.

E-F

Fillet – To remove the bone(s) from meat or fish.

Fold in – To blend a delicate frothy mixture into a heavier one so that none of the lightness and air is lost. This is best done by using a rubber spatula, turning under and bringing it up and over, rotating the bowl one-quarter turn after each motion.

Frothy – To beat until slightly foamy.

Fry – To cook in a pan or skillet with hot oil in which the oil does not totally cover the food.

G

Garnish – To decorate food with fresh herbs, flowers or candies before serving.

Glaze – To cover or coat with a sauce, syrup or egg white after application – adding both color and flavor.

Grate – To rub food against a rough perforated utensil to produce slivers, curls, chunks, etc.

Grill – To broil over charcoal or hot coals.

Grind – To produce small bits by cutting, crushing or forcing through a chopper.

H-L

Hull – To remove husk, shell or outer covering of a seed or fruit.

Infuse – To steep herbs or other flavorings in a liquid until the liquid absorbs the flavors.

Julienne – To cut vegetables, fruit, etc. into long thin matchstick strips.

Knead – To press, fold and stretch dough until smooth and elastic. (Method usually indicates a time frame and result.)

Leaven – Using a chemical leavening agent to cause batters and dough to rise. The process may occur before or during baking.

M-O

Marinate – To soak in a highly seasoned or wet solution to flavor and/or tenderize foods.

Melt – To liquefy a solid food, via the action of heat.

Mince – To cut or chop into very small, tiny pieces.

Mix – To combine foods by distributing ingredients uniformly.

Mold – To shape into a particular form.

P-Q

Parboil – To partially cook in boiling water. Most parboiled foods require additional cooking. This is good way to bring up the bright colors of vegetables when serving crudité.

Pepita – Sunflower seed.

Pit – To remove the hard inedible seed from olives, peaches, plums, etc.

Plump – To soak dried fruits, such as raisins or currants, in a liquid or liqueur until soft and plump.

Poach – To cook in a small amount of gently simmering liquid.

Purée – To reduce the pulp of cooked fruit and vegetables to a smooth and thick liquid by straining or blending.

Quesco Fresco – Fresh cheese.

R

Reduce – To boil stock, gravy or other liquid until volume is reduced, liquid has thickened, and flavor intensified.

Refresh – To place blanched and drained vegetables in cold water to halt the cooking process.

Render – To cook meat or meat trimmings at low temperature until fat melts and can be drained and strained.

Roast – To: 1) Cook by dry heat in an oven or over hot coals, or 2) Dry or parch by intense heat.

S

Sauté – To cook, stirring frequently, in a skillet containing a small amount of hot cooking oil. (Food is not immersed in oil.)

Scald – To bring milk nearly to boiling point. (Process makes yeasts breads lighter.)

Scallop – To bake with a sauce in a casserole. The food may either be mixed or layered with the sauce.

Scramble – To cook and stir simultaneously, especially with eggs.

Shred – To cut or shave food into slivers.

Shuck – To remove the husk from corn or the shell from oysters or clams.

Sift - To pass, usually dry ingredients, through a fine wire mesh to produce a uniform consistency.

Simmer – To cook in or with a liquid at or just below the boiling point.

Skim – To ladle or spoon off excess fat or scum from the surface of a liquid or pudding.

Steam – To cook with water vapor in a closed container, usually in a steamer or on a rack.

Sterilize – To purify and cleanse through exposure to intense heat.

Stew – To simmer meats or vegetables for a long period of time. Also used to tenderize meats.

Strain – To pass through a strainer or cheesecloth to break down or remove solids and/or impurities.

Stuff – To fill or pack cavities in meats, vegetables and poultry.

T

Tent – To cover roast or bird loosely with foil after roasting

Toast -   To brown and crisp by means of direct heat, or to bake until browned.

Translucent – Cook until semitransparent; clear.

Truss – To bind poultry legs and wings close to body of bird before cooking.

U-Z

Whip – To beat a mixture until air has been thoroughly incorporated and the mixture is light and fluffy, volume is greatly increased, and mixture holds its shape.

Whisk – A quick light brushing or whipping motion.

Wilt – To apply heat to cause dehydration and a droopy appearance.

188

INDEX

Notes

Notes

47828150R00114

Made in the USA
Lexington, KY
14 December 2015